THE
KIDS
ALMANAC
of

PROFESSIONAL FOOTBALL

THOMAS G. AYLESWORTH

BETTERWAY BOOKS
Cincinnati, Ohio

Among Dr. Thomas G. Aylesworth's eighty-three other books are six books
on sports:

Science at the Ball Game
Ivy League Football
The History of the World Series
The Encyclopedia of Baseball Managers
The Cubs
The Kids' World Almanac of Baseball

Cover design by Rick Britton
Cover illustration by Lafe Locke
Illustrations by Lafe Locke
Typography by Blackhawk Typesetting

97 96 95 94 93   5 4 3 2 1

Library of Congress Cataloging-in-Publication Data

Aylesworth, Thomas G.
  The Kids' almanac of professional football / Thomas G. Aylesworth.
    p. cm.
  Includes index.
  Summary: Presents trivia about football, discussing its history,
    players, records, statistics, and media coverage.
  ISBN 1-55870-266-0 : $8.95
  1. Football—Juvenile literature. 2. Football—History—Juvenile
    literature. 3. Football—Miscellanea—Juvenile literature.
  [1. Football. 2. Football—Miscellanea.] I. Title.
GV950.7.A95 1992
796.332—dc20   92-16483
                                                          CIP
                                                          AC

This book is dedicated to Pete Pihos, the only former Indiana University player in the Pro Football Hall of Fame, and to the Chicago Rockets, who could manage a record of only ten wins against twenty-seven losses in their three years of existence.

Acknowledgments

The author wishes to acknowledge:

Susan Morris, an editor with a sharp eye and immense taste.

Jay Manahan, of the National Football League office, for his kind help with the facts.

Contents

1
A Bit of History

There is a possibility that the origins of football may go back to pre-Christian times. The ancient Romans played a game called *harpastum*, which included many features of modern football and soccer. It is said that an animal bladder was used for the ball. In the words of a Roman historian: "The players divide themselves into two teams. The ball is placed on a line between them. At the two ends of the field are two other lines, beyond which the two teams strive to carry the ball."

In England, once a far outpost of the Roman Empire, the game apparently caught on. By the 1700s, the game was so violent (it was now similar to modern soccer) that a French spectator at one of the games observed, "If Englishmen call this playing, it is impossible to say what they would call fighting."

So one of the ancestors of American football was also soccer, but rugby, an offshoot of soccer, might have been the departure point for football. This game began at the Rugby School in England in 1823, through the actions of a frustrated soccer player. He was William Webb Ellis, of Rugby, who picked up the soccer ball and ran with it to the goal line. That didn't go down well with pure soccer fans, but the idea of carrying the ball as well as kicking it became accepted.

The Rugby Game was soon picked up by the students at other schools. By the late 1850s, it was being played by adults.

FOOTBALL BEGINS IN AMERICA

The first intercollegiate football game — at least on a somewhat organized level — was played on the afternoon of November 6, 1869 on Cleege Field in New Brunswick, New Jersey. The site was on the Rutgers College campus. The Rutgers opponent was the College of New Jersey, located in Princeton, a school that was later to become Princeton University.

Rutgers College was still steaming over its baseball game with the College of New Jersey three years before when the "Princeton Bloods" had thrashed them 40-2. Revenge in the form of a football game (although played with soccer rules, since modern football had not been invented) seemed to be the answer. So Rutgers sent a "defiant but courteous" written challenge to the men of Nassau Hall to engage in a football contest. The challenge was accepted, Old Nassau formed a team, and William S. Gummers, class of 1870, was elected captain.

The players wore the letters "P" and "R" on the chests of their turtleneck sweaters, the "P" standing for "Princeton Bloods" and the "R" for Rutgers.

More like soccer than modern football, there were twenty-five men from each team on the field at one time. The ball was a round rubber one. It was kicked or butted with the head. No throwing or running with the ball was allowed. The field was 360 feet by 225 feet. The score, with each goal counting one point, was Rutgers 6, College of New Jersey 4.

A week later, the same two teams met in a rematch, and the College of New Jersey won, 8-0. Thus ended the first season of American college football, with the only teams in the country tied for the national championship with one win and one loss each.

THE EARLY SPREAD OF FOOTBALL

By 1870, some teams from what was to become the Ivy League were playing soccer-style football. Columbia, Cornell, and Yale were playing on their own campuses, and Columbia played another school, Rutgers, that year. But Harvard College students began playing what was known as "The Boston Game" in 1871. It was a bit more like rugby in that players could run short distances with the ball.

In 1873, Yale, Columbia, Princeton, and Rutgers sent delegates to a meeting at the Fifth Avenue Hotel in New York City. On October 19th, as the first Intercollegiate Football Association, they drew up the rules for what remained a soccer-like game. In particular, they agreed to limit teams to a twenty-player roster — one reason that Harvard declined to participate in the association.

In May of 1874, Harvard played the first international contest in the Boston Game when a team from McGill University, of Montreal, Canada, came to Cambridge, Massachusetts. They played two games on May 14th and 15th, and played another at Montreal in the autumn of that year. The ball, unlike a soccer ball, was oval-shaped — more like a rugby football.

Another step toward modern football came in 1875, when representatives of the football clubs at Harvard and Yale met in Springfield, Massachusetts on October 16th. This group adopted rules for a new game that combined the elements of soccer and rugby. On November 13th, Yale and Harvard played their first football game under these new rules. Harvard won, 4-0.

FOOTBALL OPENS UP

The first forward pass was thrown by Yale's Walter Camp during the Princeton game of 1876. Camp, who was to go on to become the "father of college football," was being tackled when he threw the ball to Oliver Thompson, who ran it in for a touchdown. Of course, the players from Princeton protested this unorthodox maneuver. But Yale countered by pointing out that there were no rules against it. The confused umpire decided to toss a coin in order to make a decision, and the touchdown stood.

Also in 1876, on November 18th, Harvard and Yale played their first football game using an oval ball and only eleven men on each team. The next week, on November 23rd, a meeting was held at the Massasoit House in Springfield, Massachusetts. There, representatives from Columbia, Harvard, Princeton, Rutgers, and Yale formed a new Intercollegiate Football Association. They adopted rules that brought the game closer to rugby but still allowed teams to field fifteen men (causing Yale to refuse to join the association). Yale changed its mind and played Princeton in what is regarded as the first intercollegiate game under the 1876 rules. Yale won, 2-0.

Spearheaded by the twenty-two-year-old Walter Camp of Yale, a new rule committee met in 1880. The number of players on each team was reduced from fifteen to eleven. They named the team positions. The line of scrimmage was invented to replace the rugby scrum. The committee introduced the snap, since the line of scrimmage gave possession of the ball to one team. (This was the most important rule, since it allowed strategy and pre-arranged plays.) The size of the field was changed from 140 by 70 yards to 110 by 53 yards, 1 foot. (This was the maximum width that could be accommodated in Harvard Stadium.) The ball was to be kicked back to the quarterback. Finally, the team in possession of the ball retained possession unless it fumbled.

In 1881 came the first intersectional games when the University of Michigan sent its team east to play Yale, Harvard, and Princeton. This was the Michigan team that introduced the calling of signals before each play.

In 1882, college teams adopted the system of downs. The offensive team had to advance the ball five yards in three downs. If they did not, or if they lost ten yards, they had to surrender the ball to the opponents. This created the need to draw white lines across the field.

For several years since giving up the rugby rules, teams had won points by scoring touchdowns (worth two points); a goal following a touchdown, called "goal from touchdown" (worth four points); or field goals, which were drop kicked (worth five points). But in 1883 the scoring was changed to four points for a touchdown, two points for a goal from touchdown, and five points for a field goal. In 1897, the scoring was changed again to five points for a touchdown, one point for a point after touchdown (PAT), and five points for a field goal.

PROFESSIONAL FOOTBALL TAKES A BABY STEP

By the end of the 1800s, many non-collegiate teams were playing football, especially in Pennsylvania and Ohio. But these were amateur teams. Possibly the first player to be paid for playing was the brilliant guard from Yale, William "Pudge" Heffelfinger. Although his being paid was not discovered for years, he was given $500 to appear with the Allegheny Athletic Association team against the Pittsburgh Athletic Club in 1892, when he was also playing at Yale. He was, in addition, given $25 for expenses.

The first professional football game that we know about was played on August 31, 1895. In it, teams from Latrobe and Jeanette, Pennsylvania, met with Latrobe winning, 12-0. Not all the players were paid, but many of them were. John Brailler, the Jeanette quarterback, was the biggest winner, having been paid ten dollars. He later became a dentist. The credit for being the first all-pro team belongs to the Allegheny Athletic Association in 1896. But they played only two games that season.

COLLEGE FOOTBALL GOES BIG TIME

In 1901, the people in Pasadena, California, decided to hold a football game in conjunction with their Tournament of Roses Festival. They decided to go all out by inviting the University of Michigan to play Stanford University in the first Rose Bowl Game in 1902. Michigan traveled more than 2,000 miles to paste Stanford. The humiliating score was Michigan 49, Stanford 0. Because of this massacre, no more football games were played at the Tournament of Roses Festival until 1916, when Washington State beat Brown, 14-0. The committee turned to other attractions during those years, among them chariot races.

In 1905, 18 fatalities and 159 serious injuries were reported as the result of rough football games. In December, *The New York World* reported that football was the "most brutal, perilous, and unnecessary sport sanctioned by any country in the world." Horrified by a newspaper photograph of 250-pound Swarthmore guard Bob Maxwell (for whom the Maxwell Trophy was later named), bloody and beaten after a game, President Theodore Roosevelt summoned college athletic leaders to the White House and threatened to ban the sport by executive order if violence was not curbed.

In 1905, a meeting was held; college football officials decided to reform the sport. At a second meeting in December of that year, a Football Rules Committee was appointed to set up new rules.

In 1906, the new rules were put into play. They banned almost all mass formations and plays. They also increased the yardage to be gained for a first down from five yards to ten. And finally, the forward pass was legalized.

Meanwhile, also in 1906, a scandal popped up in professional football. It wasn't that many college football stars would play college ball on Saturday afternoons and then would be paid to play professionally on Sunday afternoons. That was common knowledge, although later professional football teams would ban a player who was an amateur and a professional at the same time.

Rather it was the discovery of the professional Canton (Ohio) Bulldogs betting scandal. The team was forced to disband. The Bulldogs would not reappear until 1915 with the signing of the great athlete, Jim Thorpe. With Thorpe, they won ten straight games in 1916.

In 1912, two important new rules were adopted. The first was an amendment to the scoring system. Scoring rules were changed to what we know today — six points for a touchdown, one point for a PAT, and three points for a field goal. The second was the change to new field dimensions, also the ones we know today; that is, 120 yards long and 53 yards, 1 foot wide.

THE PROFESSIONALS COME OF AGE

World War I must be given some credit for the formation of modern professional football. It was at the Rose Bowl Game of 1919 that a team representing the Great Lakes Naval Training Station trounced the Mare Island Marines squad 17-0. On the Great Lakes team were some of the men who were to shape major league football. George Halas, fresh from the University of Illinois, played end. John "Paddy" Driscoll, of Northwestern, and Harold Erickson were in the backfield. Hugh Blacklock, of what is now Michigan State, Jerry Jones, of Notre Dame, and Emmett Keefe, of Notre Dame, were also on the team.

Professional football as we know it began in 1919. At a meeting in Canton, Ohio, in July, five teams signed up for a new league, all but one of them from the state of Ohio. They were the Akron Pros (owned by Frank Neid), Canton Bulldogs (Ralph Hayes), Columbus Panhandles (Joe Carr), Dayton Triangles (Carl Storck), and Rochester, New York, Jeffersons (Leo Lyons). They called themselves the American Professional Football Association, and the fee for a league franchise was $25. All five would remain in the league at least until 1925.

Several other teams were added for the 1919 season. They were the Cleveland (Ohio) Indians, Detroit (Michigan) Heralds, Hammond (Indiana) Pros, Massillon (Ohio) Tigers, Rock Island (Illinois) Independents, Toledo (Ohio) Maroons, and a team from Wheeling, West Virginia. At the end of the season, the Canton Bulldogs, with their superstar, Jim Thorpe, claimed the championship.

But the thing that solidified the league happened on September 17, 1920. It was a meeting held in an automobile agency in Canton, Ohio. Ralph Hayes, owner of the Canton Bulldogs, also owned a Hupmobile (an early make of car) agency in the Odd Fellows' Building. The five original members of the league were ready for action as were Detroit, Hammond, Rochester, and Rock Island. Several other teams joined in, at a $100 franchise price this time.

The new teams were the Buffalo (New York) All Americans, Chicago (Illinois) Cardinals, Chicago (Illinois) Tigers, Cleveland (Ohio) Panthers, Decatur (Illinois) Staleys, and Muncie (Indiana) Flyers. The league was off to a definite, but a little shaky, start.

PRO FOOTBALL GROWS UP A BIT

The 1920 season was a raggedy one. To begin with, the league had named Jim Thorpe as its president, but he was strictly a player and not an administrator. It was soon thought that someone else should be president —

someone with a business mind — and in 1921 Joe Carr, owner of the Columbus Panhandles, was named to fill the job.

Also, the schedule was not the best that year. The championship was won by the Akron Pros, with a 6-0-3 record, who outscored their opponents by 95-7 points. But some teams played only eight games, seven games, six games, five games, three games, or even, like the Rochester and Muncie teams, only one game.

In 1921, a franchise was awarded to John E. Clair of the Acme Packing Company of Green Bay, Wisconsin. The team was to be coached by tailback Curly Lambeau. Also in 1921, George Halas's Decatur Staleys moved to Chicago; they would change their name to the Bears the next year.

Nineteen twenty-two saw the league change its name to the National Football League — a name that would stick. Still, business was not good for a few years.

Things didn't really start to turn around until 1925. It was that year that Tim Mara bought a professional football franchise, calling them the New York Giants. The team had Jim Thorpe on the squad.

But the most important thing that happened that year was that George Halas of the Chicago Bears signed the University of Illinois superrunner, Harold "Red" Grange, to play for the Bears at the end of his college season that fall. Old Number 77's first professional game wasn't much. On Thanksgiving Day, 1925, the Bears played the Cardinals to a scoreless tie.

But with Grange, the Bears staged two postseason barnstorming tours. The first tour had eight games in seven cities in an eleven-day period. The second tour scheduled nine cities ranging from Florida to the West Coast over a five-week period. All together, the barnstorming activities drew 350,000 fans.

Grange and the Bears may have saved the New York Giants from bankruptcy. The game between Chicago and New York drew 70,000 fans to New York's Polo Grounds — a record for a professional team then — and the total attendance was 5,000 more people than had viewed the Army-Navy game the week before. The receipts from this one game were $143,500.

Even better than that for the NFL was the fact that a parade of college stars followed Grange into the NFL. Among them were Stanford's Ernie Nevers, Michigan's Benny Friedman, the entire Notre Dame backfield (The Four Horsemen), and Minnesota's Bronko Nagurski.

Still, things were not going as well all over the league. By 1927, the NFL had financial difficulties and went from twenty-two to twelve teams. Leaving were the Akron Pros, Brooklyn Lions, Canton Bulldogs, Columbus Tigers, Hammond Pros, Hartford Blues, Kansas City Cowboys, Los Angeles Buccaneers, Louisville Colonels, Milwaukee Badgers, and Racine Tornadoes. The New York Yankees joined, and the Buffalo Rangers became the Buffalo Bisons.

Another problem had been the cancellation of games. Early in the league's history, games were canceled because of the weather. The problem was not that the players didn't want to play. It was that the fans would stay home. After all, there were no television contracts then, and gate receipts (or the occasional radio payments) were the only way the players would be paid. In 1929, a game contract was introduced that stated the home team had the right to cancel a game due to "inclement weather." But the cancellation had to be made at least four hours before the visiting team's train was scheduled to leave.

This was the way it stood at the end of the 1920s. Of the teams that started in the league early in the decade only the Chicago Bears, Chicago Cardinals, Green Bay Packers, and New York Giants remained. Five thousand fans was a good draw. Admission was usually not more than two or three dollars for a fifty-yard-line seat. Field goals were frequently drop kicked and forward passes were rare, except for Benny Friedman, the first truly accomplished passer.

THE SHAKY 1930s

Professional football in the 1930s was still a game in which players went both ways on offense and defense. And there were no special teams. Still, in 1930, the league felt the need to increase its player limit per team to a maximum of twenty men and a minimum of sixteen.

Of course, 1930 was a Depression year, and the New York Giants decided to do something about it. On December 14th, they played a team of Notre Dame All-Stars in an exhibition game, beating them 21-0. The take was $115,163, which was given to a New York unemployment fund.

The NFL was down to ten teams in 1931. In 1932, it had but eight teams in five cities. The cities were Chicago (Bears and Cardinals); New York (Giants, Brooklyn Dodgers, and Staten Island Stapletons); Green Bay (Packers), Portsmouth, Ohio (Spartans); and Boston (Braves).

In 1933, Staten Island had dropped out, and the Cincinnati Reds, Philadelphia Eagles, and Pittsburgh Pirates had joined the league. The NFL was split into two divisions, the East and West. Each division had five teams. The two divisional champions played each other in the first world professional football championship, with the Bears beating the Giants, 23-21.

The roster limit was increased from twenty to twenty-four men in 1935 and to thirty in 1938. Then, in 1939, the league president, Joe E. Carr, died and was replaced by Carl Storck, who had been the original owner of the Dayton Triangles in 1919.

THE FABULOUS 1940s

The T formation came to the NFL in 1940. It had been invented by the coach of Stanford University, Clark Shaughnessy, and was adopted by coaches George Halas and Ralph Jones of the Bears (with Shaughnessy as an advisor). The formation was to revolutionize football offense in the league with its counterplays, players in motion, and forward pass options.

Also in 1940, the player limit was increased to thirty-three.

Elmer Layden, a former star back for Notre Dame and the Brooklyn Horsemen, was named commissioner (the new name for president) of the NFL in 1941. Then came World War II.

Nineteen forty-two was the first full year of World War II in America, and the National Football League was to lose 638 players to the armed forces. Twenty of them were killed in the war. Of the 638, 355 were commissioned officers, and 69 were decorated for heroism. The highest decoration for bravery — the Congressional Medal of Honor — was awarded to Giants end Jack Lummus and Lions end Maurice Britt. Another hero was the former Michigan back and future star of the Los Angeles Rams, Tom Harmon (the father of actor Mark Harmon). He survived two plane crashes and credited his "football legs" with saving his life.

The NFL also raised $680,384 for War Relief charities in 1942.

In 1943, three teams were hard hit by the war. The Philadelphia Eagles and the Pittsburgh Steelers had to combine franchises, and became the "Steagles." The Cleveland Rams had to disband for the year because both owners were serving in the military. Also that year, the roster limit was reduced to twenty-eight men.

The Steelers must have been pleased with their record when combined with the Eagles as the Steagles in 1943 — they were 5-4-1 and held third place. At any rate, when the Eagles decided to go it alone in 1944, the Steelers recombined with another team, the Chicago Cardinals, to form what was known as the Card-Pitts. But the team lost all ten of their games. The Steelers became a non-hybrid team the next year.

In 1945 the roster limit went back up to thirty-three men per team.

The NFL needed a new commissioner in 1946. Over the years, many strange suggestions were made about who should be the new executive. Among them were J. Edgar Hoover, the long-time head of the Federal Bureau of Investigation; Arch Ward, the sports editor of *The Chicago Tribune* and father of the College All-Star Game; and John B. Kelly, the Olympic athlete, millionaire, and father of actress Grace Kelly. But once again the league picked a solid professional football man — Bert Bell, co-owner of the Pittsburgh Steelers.

The roster limit was increased to thirty-five men in 1948, but in 1949 it was reduced to thirty-two men.

THE EXCITING 1950s

With the addition of the Cleveland Browns, San Francisco 49ers, and Baltimore Colts to the league in 1950, the NFL changed its structure. It changed from two divisions, the East and the West, to two conferences, the American, with six teams, and the National, with seven teams.

In 1951, the Colts dropped out of the league because they were losing money. The player roster was raised to thirty-three men.

In 1953, the names American and National conferences were changed to Eastern and Western conferences. The bonus pick was eliminated from the draft of college players in 1958. In 1959, the player roster limit was raised to thirty-six men, and Commissioner Bert Bell died. Austin H. Gunsel, the league's treasurer, was appointed acting commissioner for the rest of the season.

THE CHANGING 1960s

In 1960, Alvin "Pete" Rozelle, general manager of the Los Angeles Rams, was elected commissioner of the NFL. The first million-dollar gate in history was registered in 1961 when Green Bay beat the Giants in the title game, 37-0.

The player limit was raised to thirty-seven in 1963, and the first Hall of Fame superstars were elected. In 1964, the player limit was raised once again — this time to forty.

In 1966, the NFL announced that, beginning the next year, it would divide its sixteen teams into four divisions. Two divisions under both the Western and Eastern conferences would play for the conference titles at the end of the season. Then the conference winners would play for the NFL championship and the right to meet the American Football League champion. The two leagues were also to share a common draft of college players.

AND SINCE THEN

In 1970, the NFL and AFL formally combined into the new National Football League. The league had two conferences, the American Football Conference and the National Football Conference. Each conference was to have thirteen teams, making it necessary for the Colts, Browns, and Steelers to be sent to the AFC. A system of play-offs was organized to include a wild card team from each conference.

In 1975, the roster limits were set at forty-three players. Tampa Bay and Seattle switched conferences in 1977. The Seahawks went to the AFC West and the Buccaneers to the NFC Central.

The 1978 season was extended to sixteen games, and the number of preseason games was set at four. Also, a second wild card team was allowed for each conference in the play-offs. In each conference, two wild card teams would face each other in the first postseason game each year.

In 1982, after two games, the players went out on strike. Play resumed eight weeks later with plans for a shortened season and a revised play-off schedule. Each team had played a total of nine games, and the play-offs involved the eight teams from each conference with the best records. In 1983, the roster limit was increased to forty-nine players.

2
What Does a Fan Need to Know?

Every true professional football fan needs to know many things. Probably the most important things to know are the rules.

RULES

Ever since the beginning of the NFL, there have been rule changes about equipment, tactics, winners and losers, and many other things. Here is a rundown on the history of the laws of the pro game.

1926 — College players cannot play professional football until after graduation.

1927 — The goalposts are moved to the back of the end zone.

1929 — The football is slimmed.

1933 — The goalposts are moved back to the goal line. Hash marks are introduced and located ten yards inbounds from the sidelines. The ball will be put in play here if it ends up within five yards of a sideline. The football is slimmed again, virtually eliminating the drop kick because of the untrue bounce of the pointed ends, but making the ball easier to throw and control.

1934 — Passing is legalized from anywhere behind the line of scrimmage. A player entering the game may talk to teammates. (Previously he couldn't because the league was afraid he might be bringing in a play from the coach, and coaching from the sidelines was illegal.) A penalty against the defense occurring within ten yards of its goal line is assessed at half the distance to the goal line. A runner who falls or is knocked down can get up and advance the ball; he must be held to the ground until the play is whistled dead.

1935 — The hash marks are moved to fifteen yards from the sidelines.

1938 — Roughing the passer is made a penalty.

1940 — The clipping penalty is reduced from twenty-five to fifteen yards.

1941 — A sudden death overtime period is adopted for divisional play-offs and championship games.

1943 — Free substitution is inaugurated, giving rise to platooning offense and defense. All players are to wear helmets.

1944 — Coaching from the bench is legalized.

1945 — The hash marks are moved to twenty yards in from the sidelines. Wearing socks is made mandatory.

1946 — Free substitution is outlawed. Substitution is limited to three players at a time.

1948 — The artificial tee is allowed on kickoffs.

1949 — Free substitution is restored for one year.

1950 — Free substitution is made permanent.

1955 — The ball-carrier can no longer get up and run after being knocked down.

1956 — Grabbing the face mask (except the ball-carrier's) is made illegal.

1962 — Face mask rule is broadened to include the ball-carrier.

1969 — Modified kicking shoes are outlawed.

1972 — The hash marks are brought in to be even with each goalpost upright. Regular season ties are counted as a half win, half loss.

1974 — The goalposts are moved back to the end lines. Kickoffs are moved from the forty-yard line to the thirty-five. A missed field goal from outside the twenty-yard line is brought back to the line of scrimmage. The sudden death overtime period is to last no more than fifteen minutes. It is instituted for all regular and preseason games. Crackback blocks are outlawed.

1977 — The head-slap is outlawed. Defenders can bump receivers only one time in the first five yards.

1978 — Pass blockers are allowed to extend their arms and open their hands.

1979 — Blocking below the waist on kicks is made illegal. Once a quarterback is thought to be "in the grasp" of a defender, the play is to be whistled dead. Spearing with the helmet is made a penalty.

1981 — The use of stickum to catch passes is outlawed.

1984 — A five-yard anti-celebrating penalty is installed.

1986 — Instant replay as an officiating tool debuts.

1988 — More contact between defenders and receivers is allowed.

1992 — Instant replay for officiating is eliminated.

THE OFFICIALS

But who interprets these rules?

For the first few years of the NFL there were only three officials — the referee, the umpire, and the head linesman.

Referee. He is the official who has general charge of the game. On the usual play, he takes a position in the offensive backfield ten to twelve yards behind the line of scrimmage. He watches running backs for legal motion. He watches the quarterback during and after hand-offs and then follows the runner downfield. He adjusts the final position of the ball. On pass plays, he follows the quarterback and watches the blocks near him. He rules on loose balls being fumbles or incomplete passes and on roughing the passer penalties. On field goal attempts, he stands behind the offensive line of scrimmage and rules on the kicker's actions and any contact by a defender.

Umpire. He is the official who watches for violations on the line of scrimmage. On the usual play, he takes a position four to five yards downfield in front of the weak-side tackle or strong-side guard. He rules on the players' equipment and contact on the line of scrimmage. On pass plays, he watches for illegal linemen downfield and ensures that receivers can run their routes. He also rules on blockers and assists in ruling on complete or trapped passes.

Head linesman. He is the official who marks the forward progress of the ball. On the usual play, he takes a position at the sideline on the line of scrimmage. He is responsible for offside and encroachment calls. He keeps track of the downs and is in charge of the chain crew. He also rules on plays on his side and out of bounds. He assists in determining the forward progress of the ball. On pass plays, he watches for illegal contact with the receiver past the five-yard limit and interference calls in his area.

In 1929, the NFL added another official — the field judge.

Field Judge. He is the official who watches for violations on punt returns and pass plays downfield. On the usual play, he takes a position twenty-five yards downfield, usually on the tight end side of the field. He concentrates on the tight end's potential blocks and the action against him. He times the intervals between plays on a forty-five and twenty-five second clock, as well as the time between quarters and halftime. He also rules on fair catch infractions and illegal blocks on kick and punt returns. On pass plays, he decides on catches, pass interference, and loose balls beyond the line of scrimmage.

The fifth official — the back judge — was added in 1947.

Back Judge. He is the official who watches for violations between the defensive backs and the offensive pass receivers. On the usual play, he takes a position on the same side as the line judge and twenty yards downfield. He rules on blocks by ends and backs in the secondary or contact by the players guarding them. He also rules on plays in his area along with out-of-bounds calls. On pass plays, he keys in on the wide receiver on his side, ruling on interference, pass completions, and illegal blocks.

The line judge — the sixth official— was added in 1965.

Line Judge. He is the official who watches for violations in the line and keeps the official clock. On the usual play, he takes a position straddling the line of scrimmage opposite the head linesman. He keeps track of time and is responsible for offside and encroachment calls. He also watches the blocking on his side. On pass plays, he watches for illegal contact with the receiver past the five-yard limit and interference calls in his area. He rules on the passer being behind the line of scrimmage when passing.

The seventh official — the side judge — was introduced in 1978.

Side Judge. He is the official who has the same responsibilities as the back judge. On the usual play, he takes a position on the same side as the head linesman and twenty yards downfield. He rules on blocks by the ends and backs in the secondary or contacts by players guarding them. He also rules on plays in his area, along with out-of-bounds calls. On pass plays, he keys in on the wide receiver on his side, ruling on interference, pass completions, and illegal blocks.

On field goal attempts, the back judge and field judge stand on opposite sides of the goalpost to determine if the attempt is successful. The umpire stands behind the defensive line opposite the ball. The line judge and head linesman stand at opposite ends of the offensive line. The referee stands behind the kicker to rule on the action.

Of course, from 1986 through 1991, there was also a replay official in a booth, ruling on instant replay decisions.

THE PLAYERS

But who are the men who play the game?

Quarterback. The quarterback takes the snap from center and can do one of three things with it. He can hand off the ball to one of his running backs; run with the ball himself; or pass the ball to a receiver.

Running Backs. The running back takes the ball from the quarterback and tries to gain yards by running behind the blocking of the offensive line. He can also roll out of the backfield and catch passes or stay behind to block for the quarterback on pass plays. He can even pass downfield on an option play when the quarterback hands off, or pitches, the ball to him. Most teams use two running backs, but some use only one.

Wide Receivers. These players split out wide to either side of the field. They are used to catch passes and seldom block. The fastest will be used to run deeper patterns to catch a long pass. Most teams use two wide receivers, but some use three.

Tight End. Tight ends also catch passes. They are usually bigger and slower than wide receivers, and so are often used to block on running plays.

Offensive Linemen. The *center's* job is to snap the ball to the quarterback or to the kicker on punts and field goal attempts. On either side of the center are two *guards*. Outside the guards are two *tackles*. These players, who may weigh as much as, if not more than, 300 pounds, are blockers — pushing defenders out of the way to open holes for a running back, or keeping defenders away from the quarterback on a pass play.

Defensive Linemen. These men have the job of tackling the man with the ball while avoiding blockers. On a pass play, they attempt to rush in and tackle the quarterback. Some teams use three defensive linemen (one nose tackle opposite the center and two ends). Others use four (two tackles and two ends).

Linebackers. These are usually the most versatile defensive players on defense because they must do many things: hold their ground and try to tackle the running back, drop back to cover a receiver, or try to blitz and sack the quarterback. Some teams use three linebackers (one middle and two outside). Others use four (two middle and two outside).

Defensive Backs. Teams usually have two *cornerbacks*, who line up on each side of the field outside the ends. They usually cover the wide receivers. Two other defensive backs are the *safeties*, who are positioned behind the linebackers. All four are used in pass coverage, but they also move up to make tackles on running plays. On certain running plays, a "nickel-back," or fifth defensive back, may substitute for a linebacker or lineman.

Punter. The punter usually stands twelve to fifteen yards behind the center, takes the snap, and kicks the ball as far downfield as possible for the opponents to take possession. On occasion, the punter will try to kick it out of bounds near the goal line.

Place-kicker. The place-kicker is used on kickoffs, field goals, or extra points.

Special Teams. These players are usually not starters; they play on kickoffs or punts. On the kickoff team, they try to tackle the player with the ball. On the kick-return team, they block for the player with the ball. For punts, they must do a little of both. On the punting team, players other than the punter must block defenders who want to block the kick, and then must tackle the punt return man.

THE LANGUAGE OF FOOTBALL

There is a vast ocean of words that have come into the American lexicon from football.

ANGLE BLOCK: A block in which contact is made diagonally, usually when an opponent is lined up just to the left or right of the blocker.

AREA BLOCKING: See ZONE BLOCKING.

ARTIFICIAL TURF: A huge carpet covering the field and made of artificial, grass-like fibers. It is laid over a cushion or shock-absorbing pad, which is usually applied over an asphalt base.

AUDIBLE: A verbal change of the offensive play or defensive alignment at the line of scrimmage. It is usually called by the quarterback on offense or the middle linebacker on defense.

BALANCED LINE: An offensive alignment with the same number of players on each side of the center.

BELLY SERIES: A combination of running and passing plays that begin the same way, with a hand-off or fake hand-off to a running back.

BLINDSIDE: To hit or tackle a quarterback from the side he cannot see when he is set up to throw the ball.

BLITZ: A defensive maneuver in which one or more linebackers and defensive backs charges through the offensive line to try to sack the quarterback.

BLOCK: The legal use of the shoulders or body to delay a defensive player from reaching an offensive player.

BODY BLOCK: A block that uses the side of the body rather than the shoulders. It was invented by the famed college football coach, Glenn S. "Pop" Warner.

BOMB: A long pass, especially one that scores a touchdown.

BOOTLEG: A play in which the quarterback fakes a hand-off in one direction, then hides the ball behind his hip before he runs or passes.

BROKEN PLAY: A play that doesn't go according to plan, often due to a misunderstanding between the quarterback and the running backs or receivers.

CLIP: A violation in which a player blocks or charges into an opponent, who is not a ball-carrier, below the waist and from behind.

COFFIN CORNER: One of the four corners of the field where the sideline and goal line intersect.

CORNERBACK: One of the defensive backs who line up behind and outside the linebackers in order to prevent the opponents from turning the corner on sweeps and to cover the receivers on pass plays.

COUNTER PLAY: An offensive play in which the ball-carrier runs toward the sideline in the opposite direction most players are moving.

CROSS BUCK: A play in which the quarterback hands off the ball to a running back, faking to another running back. Both run past him toward the line on diagonally-crossing paths. The play was invented by Amos Alonzo Stagg, coach of the University of Chicago.

CURL: A pass pattern in which the receiver runs straight ahead, then turns inside or outside and curls back toward the line of scrimmage.

DEAD BALL: A ball that has just been downed or travels out of bounds, rendering it out of play. The ball is also dead after a fair catch, when a time-out is called, or when a whistle is blown for a rules infraction.

DIME DEFENSE: A prevent defense that uses six defensive backs.

DOUBLE COVERAGE: The coverage of a receiver by two defensive players.

DOUBLE REVERSE: A play in which a back running toward one sideline hands off to a teammate running in the opposite direction, who then hands off to another teammate running in the original direction of the play.

DOUBLE WING: An offensive formation using an unbalanced line. The ball is snapped directly to the tailback, who is four to five yards behind the center, with the fullback about one yard in front and just to the side of him on the strong side. The double wing was the basis for modern spread formations such as the shotgun.

DOWN AND OUT: See OUT.

DOWN IN: See IN.

DRAW PLAY: A play in which the quarterback, looking for a pass rush, drops back as if to pass, then hands off to a running back who runs straight forward through the gap left by the charging defensive players.

DUMP OFF: To throw a short pass to a back when the planned receivers are covered.

ELIGIBLE RECEIVER: A player who can legally catch a forward pass. Only the backs and two ends are eligible unless a member of the opposing team touches or tips the ball. Then any offensive player can catch it. All defensive players are eligible to intercept the pass.

ENCROACHMENT: An illegal entry into the neutral zone of the line of scrimmage by part of a player's body being on or over his line of scrimmage or free kick line after the ball is ready for play and before it is snapped or kicked.

END AROUND: A reverse play in which a wide receiver or tight end turns back through the offensive backfield for a hand-off, and continues to run around the opposite side of the line. This play was invented by University of Chicago coach Amos Alonzo Stagg.

END RUN: A play in which the ball-carrier runs around one end of the line.

FACE GUARDING: The illegal obstruction or hindrance of a pass receiver by a defensive player who turns his back to the ball and waves his arms in the receiver's face to interfere with his vision. It counts as pass interference.

FACE MASK: An illegal grabbing of an opponent's face protector. If unintentional, it is a five-yard penalty. If intentional (involving twisting or pulling), it gets a fifteen-yard penalty.

FAIR CATCH: When a player about to receive a punt or kickoff raises one arm at full length and waves it, he is signaling for a fair catch. After he catches the ball, he cannot try to advance it, but no opposing player may touch him. If the ball is muffed, it is a loose ball and is treated as a fumble.

FAKE: See JUKE.

FALSE START: An illegal movement in which one or more offensive players moves after being in a set position before the ball is snapped.

FIELD POSITION: The point at which the ball is put into play. The closer the offensive team is to the opponents' goal, the better field position.

FLACK JACKET: A special lightweight padding worn like a vest to protect the ribs. It was adapted from flack jackets worn by combat helicopter crews.

FLAGRANT FOUL: A vicious, illegal foul, such as a punch or kick to the body, a nasty clip, or an intentional grabbing of the face mask. On occasion, the perpetrator is ejected from the game.

FLANK: Either side or end of a formation.

FLANKER: Also called a split end or flanker back, this is the old name for a wide receiver or other offensive player who is positioned wide of a formation. The University of Chicago coach, Amos Alonzo Stagg, invented the flanker.

FLANKER BACK: See FLANKER.

FLARE: A short pass to a back moving toward the sideline in the backfield. It is usually used as a safety valve pass when the quarterback is under pressure. It is also called a swing or swing pass.

FLAT: The part of the field on either side of a formation.

FLEA-FLICKER: Usually this trick play involves a lateral pass followed by a forward pass, a hand-off followed by a pass, or a pass followed by a lateral pass. It was invented by the coach of the University of Illinois, Bob Zuppke, in the 1920s.

FLEX DEFENSE: A formation in which two defensive linemen drop back just before the snap to protect against a run. This defense was invented by the Dallas Cowboys coach, Tom Landry, in 1977.

FLY PATTERN: A pass pattern in which the receiver runs straight downfield at full speed. It is also called a go.

FOUR-THREE DEFENSE: A defensive alignment using a four-man line, usually two tackles and two ends, and three linebackers.

FREE SAFETY: A defensive back usually positioned about ten yards behind the line of scrimmage on the weak side to cover the central area of the field against a long run or pass. Sometimes called a weak safety.

GADGET: A trick play. It is also called a razzle-dazzle play.

GO: See FLY PATTERN.

HAIL MARY: A long, low percentage pass that requires a great deal of luck for completion.

HANG TIME: The amount of time a ball is in the air between a kick and a reception, measured in seconds. The best kickers try for a hang time of close to five seconds.

HASH MARKS: Two rows of lines paralleling the sidelines. All plays start between or on the hash marks.

HITCH AND GO: A pass pattern in which the receiver runs straight downfield a short distance, fakes a hitch to the outside, and then continues downfield at full speed.

HOLDING: Illegally grabbing, hooking, grasping, or obstructing an opponent with the hands or arms, except for the ball-carrier.

HUDDLE: A meeting of the offensive team behind the line of scrimmage in which signals and instructions for the next play are given, usually by the quarterback. It was invented by University of Chicago Coach Amos Alonzo Stagg.

HURRY-UP OFFENSE: See TWO-MINUTE DRILL.

I FORMATION: An offensive formation in which the fullback and the tailback (both running backs) are positioned in line behind the quarterback with the third back playing wide as a receiver. The formation was invented by the coach of the Virginia Military Institute, Tom Nugent, in the 1950s.

ILLEGAL MOTION: An infraction in which an offensive player other than the one man in motion fails to come to a complete stop in a set position and remain motionless for one full second before the snap of the ball.

ILLEGAL PROCEDURE: A violation in which the offense does not have seven players on the line of scrimmage or if an offensive player moves before the ball is snapped. Illegal procedure is also called if the offense or defense has more than eleven players on the field.

IN: A pass pattern in which a receiver runs straight downfield, then cuts sharply to the inside for a pass. This is also called a down in or a square in.

INELIGIBLE RECEIVER: Offensive linemen between the two ends are not permitted to catch a forward pass, and they cannot advance beyond the point where physical contact is broken with the opponent blocked from the initial line change until the ball is thrown.

INTENTIONAL GROUNDING: An illegal play in which the passer, unable to find a receiver, deliberately throws the ball to the ground, into a player behind the line, or out of bounds.

INTERFERENCE: A violation in which the pass receiver or pass defender is blocked, tackled, or shoved while the ball is still in the air. In defensive interference, the offense gets the ball at the spot of the foul and receives a first down. In offensive interference, the offense is penalized fifteen yards and a down.

JUKE: To make a motion or movement in a certain direction in order to deceive the opponent. This is also called a fake.

KEEPER: A play in which the quarterback keeps the ball and runs with it, usually after faking a hand-off. The play was invented by the University of Chicago coach, Amos Alonzo Stagg.

LATE HIT: The illegal act of diving on or running into an opponent after he is down or out of play, or after the ball is dead.

LATERAL PASS: A pass thrown in any direction other than forward. Any player is eligible to catch it, but if it hits the ground inbounds, the ball is still in play and may be recovered by either team. This pass was invented by the University of Chicago coach, Amos Alonzo Stagg.

LINES OF SCRIMMAGE: Two imaginary lines aligning with the spot where the previous play ended. The defensive line of scrimmage starts behind the end of the ball closest to their own goal line. The offensive line of scrimmage starts behind the other point of the ball. The area between the two lines of scrimmage (the length of the football) is the neutral zone.

LOOK-IN PASS: A quick pass to a receiver who has run diagonally across the middle.

MAN-FOR-MAN COVERAGE: A defensive coverage in which each receiver is guarded by one defensive player.

MAN IN MOTION: The movement of a single offensive player, after assuming a set position for one second following the huddle or a shift, in a lateral or backward direction behind the line of scrimmage at the snap of the ball. The man in motion was invented by the University of Chicago coach, Amos Alonzo Stagg.

MIDDLE GUARD: See NOSE GUARD.

MULTIPLE OFFENSE: An offense in which different kinds of plays can be run from a single formation. It was invented by the Michigan State University coach, Biggie Munn.

NAKED REVERSE: A play in which all the blockers move in the original direction of the play, leaving the quarterback to hand off to a runner who is without blockers, but with an open field if the defense has shifted with the offensive team.

NEUTRAL ZONE: An imaginary area between the lines of scrimmage. There is a line of scrimmage at either end of the football. The neutral zone was introduced in 1903 by former Harvard team captain Bert Walters. Before that, opposing linemen were separated only by an imaginary line through the center of the ball.

NICKEL DEFENSE: A prevent defense in which five backs are used, the extra back replacing a linebacker. The nickel defense was invented by Stanford University coach Clark Shaughnessy.

NOSE GUARD: A defensive lineman usually positioned in the middle of the line opposite the defensive center. He is also called the middle guard.

OFF: Outside of a specified offensive lineman.

OFFSIDE: A violation in which a player crosses the line of scrimmage or the free kick line before the ball is put into play. The center on a scrimmage down or the holder and kicker on a free kick down are the only players permitted to be partially in the neutral zone when the ball is put into play. Other players on a scrimmage play are not offside if they get back onside before the ball is snapped.

ONSIDE KICK: A kickoff in which the kicking team attempts to maintain possession of the ball by recovering the kick after it travels a required ten yards. The onside kick was invented by University of Chicago coach Amos Alonzo Stagg.

OPTION PLAY: An offensive play in which the quarterback runs along the line of scrimmage with the choice of keeping the ball, passing it, or tossing it off to a running back.

OUT: A pass pattern in which a receiver runs straight downfield, then cuts to the outside. It is also called a down and out or a square out.

OVERSHIFT: A defensive alignment in which all or some of the defensive linemen shift one position toward the strong side of an unbalanced line.

PERSONAL FOUL: A foul in which a player strikes, kicks, knees, spears, trips, clips, charges into, piles on, or grabs the face mask of an opponent. This can also be called unnecessary roughness or unsportsmanlike conduct.

PILING ON: Illegally jumping on a downed ball-carrier or into a pile of defensive players on a downed ball-carrier.

PITCHOUT: A lateral pass toward the outside behind the line of scrimmage.

PLACE KICK: A kick made when the ball is in a fixed position on the ground, on a kicking tee, or held by a teammate. It is usually used in kickoffs, field goals (without a tee), and extra point attempts (without a tee). It was invented by University of Chicago coach Amos Alonzo Stagg.

PLAY ACTION PASS: A pass play that is disguised to look like a running play, with a running back taking a fake hand-off and following blockers as though carrying the ball. The play action pass was popularized by Lions quarterback Bobby Lane in the 1950s.

POCKET: An area back of the line of scrimmage from which the quarterback passes as he is protected by blockers who drop back from the line to form a cup-like barrier.

POST PATTERN: A pass pattern in which a receiver runs downfield near the sideline, then cuts inside toward the goalpost.

POWER I: A version of the I formation in which the fourth back lines up in the backfield beside the fullback instead of as a wide receiver. The formation was invented by the University of Southern California coach, John McKay.

POWER SWEEP: A running play in which both guards pull out of the line at the snap to lead a sweep around one end.

PREVENT DEFENSE: A formation that includes extra defensive backs to provide additional protection against an expected long pass.

PRO SET: Any of several variations of the T formation in which one back lines up as a wide receiver on one side of the formation and the end on the other side is positioned as a split end.

QUARTERBACK DRAW: A play in which the quarterback, after dropping back as if to pass, runs straight forward through the onrushing defenders.

QUARTERBACK SNEAK: A play for short yardage in which the quarterback takes the snap and immediately runs over the center.

QUICK COUNT: A shorter than usual sequence of signals called by the quarterback to catch the defense off-guard.

QUICK KICK: A surprise punt made on a down before fourth down from a normal appearing pass or run formation.

QUICK OPENER: A play for short yardage in which a running back takes a quick hand-off from the quarterback and plunges through a hole in the line opened by blockers.

RAZZLE-DAZZLE PLAY: A tricky and unconventional play, such as a double or triple reverse, intended to deceive or confuse the opponents. See GADGET.

RED DOG: A pass rush or blitz by linebackers.

RED ZONE: The area inside the opponents' twenty-yard line, where it is more difficult to advance the ball since the defense can be more concentrated because they have a smaller area to defend.

REVERSE: An offensive play in which a back running laterally toward one sideline hands off to a teammate going the opposite way. It was invented by University of Chicago coach Amos Alonzo Stagg.

ROLL OUT: To move laterally behind the line after receiving the snap before passing, pitching out, or running with the ball. The movement is done by the quarterback.

ROUGHING THE KICKER: A foul in which a defensive player charges into the kicker on a punt, field goal attempt, or extra point attempt when he is in the act of kicking. It is not a foul if contact is made after blocking or deflecting the kick, is the result of being blocked into the kicker, or is the result of the kicker's momentum.

ROUGHING THE PASSER: A foul in which a defensive player charges into, blocks, or tackles the passer after it is clear that the pass has been thrown.

SACK: The tackle of a quarterback before he can throw a pass.

SAFETY: A two-point score given to the defensive team when an offensive player in control of the ball is downed or goes out of bounds on or behind his own goal line. A safety is also called when an offensive player loses control of a ball that is downed or goes out of bounds on or behind the goal line. No safety is awarded when a player receives a kick or intercepts a pass behind his goal line and does not try to run it out of the end zone.

SAFETY VALVE: A short pass dumped off to a back in the flat when a quarterback cannot find an open receiver downfield.

SCREEN PASS: A play in which the quarterback retreats behind the line of scrimmage and then tosses a short pass to a receiver waiting in the flat behind several blockers.

SEAM: An undefended area between two zones of a zone defense.

SHOTGUN: A spread formation for passing in which the quarterback is several yards behind the center to receive the snap. It was invented by 49ers coach Red Hickey in 1960.

SHOVEL PASS: An underhand pass that is often used for a pitchout on a lateral pass.

SINGLE WING: An offensive formation using an unbalanced line in which the ball is snapped directly to either the tailback, positioned four to five yards behind the center, or the fullback, positioned about a yard in front and just to the side of him on the strong side. The remaining two backs line up on the strong side, the quarterback as a blocking back behind the guard or tackle, and the other back as a wingback behind and just outside the end. The formation was invented by Glenn "Pop" Warner about 1906.

SLOTBACK: A back positioned behind the space between a tackle and an end.

SPEAR: A foul in which the helmet is deliberately driven into a player who is down, held by a teammate and going down, or out of the play.

SPECIAL TEAM: A squad called into a game for one play in special circumstances. There are special teams for kickoffs, punts, field goals, and extra point attempts. It is also called a suicide squad.

SPLIT END: An offensive player who stands on the side of the line of scrimmage opposite the tight end and several yards from the tackle. He is usually used as a pass receiver. He is also called a flanker, wide receiver, or spread end.

SPLIT T: A T formation in which the line is spread out, with the tackles and ends lining up wider than usual. The formation was invented by the coach of the University of Missouri, Don Faurot, in 1941.

SPOT PASS: A pass that is thrown to a predetermined spot rather than to a receiver.

SPREAD END: See SPLIT END.

SPREAD FORMATION: An offensive formation in which the backs are spread out, such as in the double wing or shotgun. The formation was used by George Halas's Decatur Staleys as early as 1920.

SQUARE IN: See IN.

SQUARE OUT: See OUT.

SQUIB KICK: A kickoff that is intentionally kicked low so that it will bounce erratically along the ground and be difficult for the receiving team to handle.

STACK: A formation in which players line up one behind the other to disguise the direction in which they will move.

STIFF ARM: See STRAIGHT ARM.

STRAIGHT ARM: Legally to use the palm of the hand to ward off or hold off at arm's length a would-be tackler. It is also called stiff arm.

STRONG SAFETY: A defensive back positioned opposite the strong side of the offensive line. He is responsible for defending against a long run or pass. He is also called the tight safety.

STRONG SIDE: The side of an unbalanced line on which the tight end is positioned.

SUDDEN DEATH: An extra fifteen-minute period of play to decide the winner of a game tied at the end of regulation play. The first team to score is the winner.

SUICIDE SQUAD: See SPECIAL TEAM.

SWEEP: A running play around either end and behind the blockers.

T FORMATION: An offensive formation in which the backs are positioned roughly in the shape of a T, with the quarterback just behind the center to take the snap directly, and the fullback several yards straight back, between and slightly behind the two halfbacks. The formation was developed in the late 1930s by the Bears assistant coach, Ralph Jones, and the Stanford University coach, Clark Shaughnessy.

TAILBACK: The deepest positioned offensive back in formations such as the I and the single wing.

THREE-FOUR DEFENSE: A defensive alignment that uses a three-man line and four linebackers.

TIGHT END: The offensive player who lines up near the tackle. He may either block or receive a pass.

TIGHT SAFETY: See STRONG SAFETY.

TOUCHBACK: A situation in which a ball that is kicked, punted, or passed by one team travels over the other team's goal line and is deliberately downed there by the other team, or goes out of bounds. After a touchback, the team into whose end zone the ball traveled puts the ball into play at its own twenty-yard line.

TRAP: A running play in which the offensive line allows a defensive lineman into the backfield and blocks him from the side. The ball-carrier then runs through the hole left by the blocked lineman.

TRIPLE OPTION: An offensive play that begins the same way on every down in which the quarterback has three choices: he can hand off to the fullback for a run through the line, pitch the ball out to a halfback for a run to the outside, or keep the ball to run or pass it himself.

TURNOVER: The loss of possession of the ball by a team because of a misplay or an error.

TWO-MINUTE DRILL: An offensive strategy in which several plays are called in one huddle to save time during the end of a half or a game. It is also called the hurry-up offense or two-minute offense.

TWO-MINUTE OFFENSE: See TWO-MINUTE DRILL.

TWO-MINUTE WARNING: The referee's notification to the coaches that only two minutes remain in the first half or the game.

UNBALANCED LINE: An offensive alignment in which there are more linemen on one side of the center than the other. It was invented by the University of Chicago coach, Amos Alonzo Stagg.

UNNECESSARY ROUGHNESS: See PERSONAL FOUL.

UNSPORTSMANLIKE CONDUCT: See PERSONAL FOUL.

VEER OFFENSE: An offense based on the triple option run from a three-end formation.

WEAK SAFETY: See FREE SAFETY.

WEAK SIDE: The side on an unbalanced line having fewer players.

WIDE RECEIVER: See FLANKER.

WING T FORMATION: A variation of the T formation in which one halfback lines up on the flank as a wingback.

WISHBONE: A variation of the T formation, which uses an unbalanced line. The halfbacks are positioned on either side of and slightly behind the fullbacks. It was invented by the University of Texas coach, Darrell Royal, in 1968. It is also called the wishbone T.

WISHBONE T: See WISHBONE.

ZONE BLOCKING: A strategy in which specific zones are assigned to defensive players to protect. Any opponent entering the zone is blocked, as opposed to the blocking of assigned players.

ZONE COVERAGE: A defensive strategy to protect against a pass. Specific areas on zones are assigned to defensive players, and any opponent entering the zone is guarded. The coverage was first used by Packers Coach Earl "Curly" Lambeau and Lions Coach Gus Dorais in the 1930s.

3
The Most Memorable

The NFL did not keep statistics until 1933, so some of the figures about mosts and leasts, oldest and youngest, and other items may not be completely true. For example, the coldest game in history may just be a guess. In 1981, playing in Cincinnati, the Bengals beat the Chargers 27-7, fighting a temperature of 9° below zero and a wind chill of 59° below. Maybe the wind chill has been lower in Green Bay or in Minneapolis when the Vikings played outdoors, but no record of that exists.

THE BEST AND THE WORST

The Best Team: The Miami Dolphins, with their celebrated "No Name Defense" and their stellar quarterback, future Hall of Famer Bob Griese, finished the 1972 season with an unprecedented 14-0 record. By the time they had beaten the Steelers 21-17 in the AFC Championship Game and the Redskins 14-7 in Super Bowl VII, they were 16-0 for the season.

The Worst Team: You can take your pick on this one, depending on whether you want the weakest team or the most miserable team.

The weakest team was probably the Cincinnati Reds of 1933 and 1934. In 1933, while they had a record of 3-6-1, they scored only thirty-eight points all year (that included a mere three touchdowns) while giving up 110 points. But 1934 was even worse. That year they scored only ten points and gave up 243. Suspended by the league for not paying their debts, they dropped out of the NFL after eight games that year.

On the other hand, there were the Dallas Texans of 1952. Previously they had been the New York Yanks. But no one was interested in them. They opened the season against the Giants and only 17,499 people showed up. On Thanksgiving Day, they met the Bears in Akron, Ohio. This was a doubleheader, and it had a full house for the first game — a game between two area high schools. Few people, however, stayed around for the second game. Although the Texans beat the Bears, only a few hundred saw it. Before that game, the team had played seven games without winning a single one, and the owners decided the crowds were so small in Dallas that they would finish their season on the road. The Texans ended up with a 1-11 record, having scored 182 points against the opponents' 427. That was their only year in Dallas, and twenty of their players never played pro football again.

THE OLDEST AND YOUNGEST

The Oldest Coach: When George Halas of the Bears finally retired from coaching in 1967, he was seventy-two.

The Youngest Coach: When David Shula was named Bengals coach in 1991, he was thirty-two years, seven months old — younger than several of his players.

The Oldest Player: George Blanda, who had played quarterback for the Bears, Colts, Oilers, and Raiders, retired two weeks short of his forty-ninth birthday.

The Youngest Player: In 1936, Bears guard Dan Fortmann was a mere twenty years old.

THE FASTEST AND THE SLOWEST

The Fastest Passer: Quarterback Bob Waterfield of the Cleveland/Los Angeles Rams threw a sixty-yard pass that was clocked at 68.18 miles per hour.

The Slowest Player: Lineman Ed "Pud" "Tubby" Sauer of the Dayton Triangles was only five feet, ten inches tall, yet he weighed in at nearly 300 pounds. Compare that with today's biggest player — William "The Refrigerator" Perry, defensive tackle for the Bears, who was estimated to be some 360 pounds in 1991, but is six feet, two inches tall.

THE LONGEST AND SHORTEST

The Longest Game: In 1971, the divisional play-off game in the AFC lasted eighty-two minutes, forty seconds. It was played on Christmas Day and the Dolphins beat the Chiefs 27-24.

The Longest Pass: In 1939, Redskins quarterback Frank Filchock lined up in kick formation, but flipped a pass to Andy Farkas, who ran for ninety-nine yards for a touchdown against the Steelers.

The Longest Punt: In 1969, Steve O'Neal of the Jets punted ninety-eight yards against the Broncos.

The Longest Contract: In 1964, Tom Landry, the coach of the Dallas Cowboys, was given a ten-year contract.

The Longest Series Played for Charity: The College All-Star Game with the champion of the NFL lasted forty-two years and raised more than three million dollars for *Chicago Tribune* charities.

The Longest Play: In the early days of professional football, a team from Chillicothe, Ohio, played the Texas All-Stars. Chillicothe fumbled the ball across the Texas goal line. A Texas back picked it up and raced with it the length of the field, but fumbled and watched the ball roll across the Chillicothe goal line. A Chillicothe back grabbed the ball in his own end zone and ran the length of the field until he was tackled one yard from where the ball had been put into play. The ball traveled over 200 yards and crossed both goal lines, yet it lost a yard and gained a first down.

The Tallest Player: Richard Sligh, a defensive tackle for the Oakland Raiders, was seven feet tall.

The Shortest Touchdown Pass: On October 9, 1960, quarterback Eddie LeBaron of the Cowboys tossed a pass to Richard Bielski for a touchdown. The yardage was two inches.

The Shortest Career: In 1929, Jack "Soapy" Shapiro of the Staten Island Stapletons played only one game.

The Shortest Passing Career: In 1941, Charles Seabright of the Cleveland Rams threw only one pass and it was intercepted.

The Shortest Punting Career: In 1941, Hugh Gallarneau, the Bears rookie back, punted against the Cardinals. The kick was blocked and he never punted again.

LARGEST AND SMALLEST

The Largest Player: Lions middle guard Les Bingaman weighed 350 pounds.

The Smallest Player: Jack "Soapy" Shapiro, of the Staten Island Stapletons, was only five feet, one-half inch tall and weighed only 121 pounds.

The Largest Crowd at a Regular Season Game: In 1957, the Rams beat the 49ers in the Los Angeles Coliseum, 37-24, before 102,368 fans.

The Largest Victory Margin: The Bears beat the Redskins 73-0 in the 1940 championship game. (See Chapter 12.)

The Largest Super Bowl Victory Margin: The 49ers beat the Broncos 55-10, for a forty-five-point margin, in Super Bowl XXIV in 1989.

TEAM RECORDS

Most League Championships: Green Bay — 10

Most Super Bowl Championships: Pittsburgh, San Francisco — 4

COACHING RECORDS

Most Seasons as Coach: George Halas, Bears — 40

Most Championships as Coach: George Halas, Bears; Curly Lambeau, Packers — 6

INDIVIDUAL RECORDS

Rushing, Lifetime

Most Rushing Attempts: Walter Payton, Bears — 3,838

Most Yards Gained: Walter Payton, Bears — 16,726

Best Yardage per Rush: Jim Brown, Browns — 5.2

Best Yardage per Rush in a Season: Beattie Feathers, Bears — 9.9 (1934)

Most Yards Gained in a Season: Eric Dickerson, Rams — 2,105 (1984)

Most Yards Gained in a Game: Walter Payton, Bears — 275 (1977)

Most One-Hundred-Yard Games in a Season: Eric Dickerson, Rams — 12 (1984)

Most One-Hundred-Yard Games in a Career: Walter Payton, Bears — 77

Most Rushing Touchdowns in a Career: Walter Payton, Bears — 110

Most Touchdowns Rushing in a Season: John Riggins, Redskins — 24 (1983)

Most Touchdowns Rushing in a Game: Ernie Nevers, Cardinals — 6 (1929)

Most Rushing Attempts in a Season: James Wilder, Buccaneers — 407 (1984)

Most Rushing Attempts in a Game: Jamie Morris, Redskins — 45 (1988)

Longest Run from Scrimmage — Tony Dorsett, Cowboys — 99 yards (1983)

Passing, Lifetime

Most Passing Attempts: Fran Tarkenton, Vikings, Giants, Vikings — 6,467

Most Passing Completions: Fran Tarkenton, Vikings, Giants, Vikings — 3,686

Most Passing Yards: Joe Montana, 49ers — 34,995

Most Yards Gained in a Season: Dan Marino, Dolphins — 5,084 (1984)

Most Yards Gained in a Game: Norm Van Brocklin, Rams — 554 (1951)

Most Touchdown Passes in a Career: Fran Tarkenton, Vikings, Giants, Vikings — 342

Most Touchdowns Passing in a Season: Dan Marino, Dolphins — 48 (1984)

Most Touchdowns Passing in a Game: Sid Luckman, Bears (1943); Adrian Burk, Eagles (1954); George Blanda, Oilers (1961); Y.A. Tittle, Giants (1962); Joe Kapp, Vikings (1969) — 7

Most Passing Attempts in a Season: Dan Marino, Dolphins — 523 (1986)

Most Passing Attempts in a Game: George Blanda, Oilers — 68 (1964)

Most Passes Completed in a Season: Dan Marino, Dolphins — 378 (1986)

Most Passes Completed in a Game: Richard Todd, Jets — 42 (1980)

Most Consecutive Passes Completed: Joe Montana, 49ers — 22 (1987)

Most Consecutive Games with Touchdown Passes: Johnny Unitas, Baltimore Colts — 47

Receiving, Lifetime

Most Receptions in a Career: Steve Largent, Seahawks — 819

Most Yards Receiving in a Career: Steve Largent, Seahawks — 13,089

Most Yardage per Reception: Charlie Joiner, Oilers, Bengals, Chargers — 16.2

Most Yards Gained in a Season: Charley Hennigan, Oilers — 1,746 (1961)

Most Yards Gained in a Game: Willie Anderson, Rams — 336 (1989)

Most Pass Receptions in a Season: Art Monk, Redskins — 106 (1984)

Most Pass Receptions in a Game: Tom Fears, Rams (1950) — 18

Most Consecutive Games with Pass Receptions: Steve Largent, Seahawks — 177

Most Touchdown Receptions in a Career: Steve Largent, Seahawks — 100

Most Touchdown Receptions in a Season: Jerry Rice, 49ers — 22 (1987)

Most Touchdown Receptions in a Game: Bob Shaw, Cardinals (1950); Kellen Winslow, Chargers (1981); Jerry Rice, 49ers (1990) — 5

Scoring, Lifetime

Most Points in a Career: George Blanda, Bears, Oilers, Raiders — 2,002

Most Points in a Season: Paul Hornung, Packers — 176 (1960)

Most Points in a Game: Ernie Nevers, Chicago Cardinals — 40 (1929)

Most Touchdowns in a Season: John Riggins, Redskins — 24 (1984)

Most Touchdowns in a Game: Ernie Nevers, Chicago Cardinals (1929); Dub Jones, Browns (1951); Gale Sayers, Bears (1965) — 6

Most PATs in a Season: Uwe von Schamann, Dolphins — 66 (1984)

Most Consecutive PATs: Tommy Davis, 49ers — 234

Most Field Goals in a Game: Jim Bakker, St. Louis Cardinals (1967); Rich Karlins, Vikings (1989) — 7

Most Field Goals in a Season: Ali Haji-Sheikh, Giants — 35 (1966)

Most Field Goals Attempted in a Season: Bruce Gossett, Rams (1966); Curt Knight, Redskins (1971) — 49

Most Field Goals Attempted in a Game: Jim Bakker, St. Louis Cardinals — 9 (1967)

Most Consecutive Field Goals Made: Kevin Butler, Bears — 24 (1988-89)

Most Consecutive Games with Field Goal Scored: Fred Cox, Vikings — 31 (1968-70)

Longest Field Goal: Tom Dempsey, Saints — 63 yards (1970)

Highest Field Goal Completion Percentage in a Season: Mark Moseley, Redskins (1982); Eddie Murray, Lions (1988 and 1989) — 95.2

Pass Interceptions

Most Passes for Interceptions in a Game: Jim Hardy, Chicago Cardinals — 8 (1950)

Most Passes for Interceptions in a Season: George Blanda, Oilers — 42 (1962)

Most Passes for Interceptions in a Career: George Blanda, Bears, Oilers, Raiders — 277

Most Consecutive Games Passing for Interceptions: Tom Morrow, Oakland Raiders — 8 (1962-63)

Most Consecutive Pass Attempts without an Interception: Bernie Kosar, Browns — 308 (1991)

Most Interceptions in a Season: Dick "Nighttrain" Lane, Rams (1952); Al Worley, Redskins (1968) — 14

Most Interceptions in a Career: Paul Krause, Redskins, Vikings — 81

Punting

Most Punts in a Game: Cub Buck, Packers — 19 (1923)

Most Punts in a Career: Dave Jennings, Giants, Jets — 1,154

Most Punts in a Season: Bob Parsons, Bears — 114

Highest Punting Average in a Season: Sammy Baugh, Redskins — 54.04 yards (1940)

Highest Punting Average in a Career: Sammy Baugh, Redskins — 45 yards

Kickoff Returns

Most Kickoff Return Yardage in a Career: Ron Smith, Bears, Falcons, Rams, Bears, Chargers, Oakland Raiders — 6,922

Most Kickoff Return Yardage in a Season: Buster Rhymes, Vikings — 1,345 (1985)

Most Kickoff Return Yardage in a Game: Wally Triplett, Lions — 294 (1950)

Highest Average Kickoff Return Yardage in a Career: Gale Sayers, Bears — 30.56

Highest Average Kickoff Return Yardage in a Season: Travis Williams, Packers — 41.1 (1967)

Most Touchdowns Scored on Kickoff Returns in a Career: Ollie Matson, Chicago Cardinals; Gale Sayers, Bears; Travis Williams, Packers, Rams — 6

Most Touchdowns Scored on Kickoff Returns in a Season: Travis Williams, Packers (1967); Cecil Turner, Bears (1970) — 4

Most Touchdowns Scored on Kickoff Returns in a Game: Tim Brown, Eagles (1966); Travis Williams, Packers (1967); Ron Brown, Los Angeles Rams (1985) — 2

Most Kickoff Returns in a Career: Ron Smith, Bears, Falcons, Los Angeles Rams, Bears, Chargers, Oakland Raiders — 275

Most Kickoff Returns in a Season: Drew Hill, Rams — 60 (1981)

Longest Kickoff Return: Al Carmichael, Packers (1956); Noland Smith, Chiefs (1967); Roy Green, St. Louis Cardinals (1979) — 106 yards

Punt Returns

Most Yardage Returning Punts in a Career: Billy "Whiteshoes" Johnson, Oilers, Falcons, Redskins — 3,317

Most Yardage Returning Punts in a Season: Fulton Walker, Dolphins, Raiders — 692 (1985)

Most Yardage Returning Punts in a Game: Leroy Irvin, Rams — 207 (1981)

Highest Punt Return Average in a Career: Billy "Whiteshoes" Johnson, Oilers, Falcons, Redskins — 13.16 yards

Highest Punt Return Average in a Season: Herb Rich, Baltimore Colts — 23 yards (1950)

Most Touchdowns Scored on Punt Returns in a Career — Jack Christiansen, Lions; Rick Upchurch, Broncos — 8

Most Punt Returns in a Career: Billy "Whiteshoes" Johnson, Oilers, Falcons, Redskins — 282

Most Punt Returns in a Season: Danny Reece, Buccaneers — 70 (1979)

Miscellaneous Records

Most Fumbles in a Season: Dave Krieg, Seahawks (1989); Warren Moon, Oilers (1990) — 18

Most Fumbles in a Game: Len Dawson, Chiefs — 7 (1964)

Most Fumbles Recovered in a Career: Jim Marshall, Vikings — 29

Most Sacks in a Career: Lawrence Taylor, Giants — 121.5

Most Sacks in a Season: Mark Gastineau, Jets — 22 (1984)

Most Sacks in a Game: Derrick Thomas, Chiefs — 7 (1990)

Most Times Sacked in a Career: Fran Tarkenton, Vikings, Giants, Vikings — 483

Most Times Sacked in a Season: Randall Cunningham, Eagles — 72 (1986)

Most Rushing Yardage by a Quarterback in a Career: Fran Tarkenton, Vikings, Giants, Vikings — 4,703

Most Seasons as an Active Player: George Blanda, Bears, Oilers, Oakland Raiders — 26

Most Consecutive Games Played: Jim Marshall, Browns, Vikings — 282

Most Career Touchdowns: Don Hutson, Packers — 99

Most Touchdowns in a Season: Don Hutson, Packers (1942); Elroy "Crazylegs" Hirsch, Rams (1951); Bill Groman, Oilers (1961) — 17

MISCELLANEOUS TEAM RECORDS

Highest Scoring Play-off Game: Chargers 41, Dolphins 38 (1981 OT)

Highest Scoring Super Bowl: Steelers 35, Cowboys 31 (1979)

Most Points by Two Teams in One Game: Giants 72, Redskins, 41 (1966)

Most Points Scored by a Losing Team: Chiefs — 48 (1983, Seahawks 51, Chiefs 48 in OT)

Most Seasons Leading the League in Fewest Points Allowed: Bears — 9 (1932, 1936, 1937, 1942, 1948, 1963, 1985, 1986, 1988)

Fewest Points Allowed in a Season: Bears — 44 (1932)

Fewest Points Scored in a Complete Season: Giants — 20 (1927)

Most Consecutive Shutouts: Lions — 7 (1934)

Most Consecutive Winning Seasons: Cowboys — 19

Most Fumbles in a Season: Bears — 56 (1938)

Fewest Fumbles in a Season: Browns — 8 (1959)

Most Yards Penalized in a Season: Oakland Raiders — 1,274 (1969)

4
The Superstars

From Jim Thorpe to Mark Rypien, the National Football League has been filled with superstars. Most of them are men who were standouts on the field, of course. But several were men who were standouts in the real world, too.

In the early days, players played sixty minutes on both offense and defense. Paul Hornung of the Packers rushed for yardage and also kicked PATs. Jerry Kramer of the Packers played guard and kicked field goals. Others scored and also kicked extra points, such as Gene Mingo (Broncos, Redskins, Saints, Steelers), Bobby Layne (Bears, Bulldogs, Lions, Steelers), Gordy Soltau (Boston Patriots), Doak Walker (Lions), Pat Harder (Chicago Cardinals, Lions), Ted Frisch (Packers), and Don Hutson (Packers). And Lou "The Toe" Groza (Browns), the Hall of Fame field goal wizard, also played tackle.

Some players became great humanitarians. Alan Page, the defensive tackle of the Vikings, struck a blow for education when he was inducted into the Hall of Fame in 1988. At the induction ceremony, inductees are introduced by a person of their choice — most often by a former coach or teammate. Page asked one of his old teachers from Canton, Ohio, to do the job for him. Page went on to get a law degree and now serves as an assistant attorney general in Minnesota. He also ran for the state supreme court in 1992. In his spare time, he runs his own educational foundation for "children of color." He awards $1,000 grants to high school graduates on the condition that they act as mentors and role models in their neighborhoods in Minneapolis and St. Paul.

PUBLIC SERVANTS

Several league veterans have gone on to be leaders in government and the law. Probably the most outstanding is Byron "Whizzer" White. After an outstanding career at the University of Colorado, White played running back in the NFL for the Steelers (1938) and the Lions (1940-41). Named as a Deputy United States Attorney General in 1961, he was appointed a United States Supreme Court Associate Justice in 1962, where he still serves.

Jack Kemp, from Occidental College, was a star quarterback for the Steelers (1957), Los Angeles/San Diego Chargers (1960-62), and Bills (1962-67, 1969). He was elected to the House of Representatives from the state of New York in 1971, and his name was occasionally suggested as a presidential candidate. He is currently the United States Secretary of Housing and Urban Development.

Ed King, who played for Boston College and later was a guard for the Bills (1948-49) and the Baltimore Colts (1950), served as governor of Massachusetts from 1979 to 1983.

Nick Buoniconti was a Notre Dame linebacker. After playing for the Boston Patriots (1962-68) and the Dolphins (1969-74, 1976), in 1982 he became the Democratic Party chairman for Dade County, Florida.

Lavie Dilweg was a back for Marquette University and played for the Milwaukee Badgers (1926) and the Packers (1927-34). Later he served in the House of Representatives from 1943 to 1945, representing the state of Wisconsin.

Bill Dudley, who was a back from the University of Virginia, played for the Steelers (1942, 1945-46), Lions (1947-49), and Redskins (1950-51, 1953). He then served in the General Assembly of the state of Virginia from 1966 to 1974.

Yale Lary, who played for Texas A&M, went on to become a star back for the Lions (1952-53, 1956-64). He began his term of office in the Texas State Legislature (1959-62) while he was still in the NFL.

There have been some presidents who participated in football, but none played professionally. Woodrow Wilson coached football at Wesleyan University in Middletown, Connecticut, in 1889. And Dwight D. Eisenhower was a football star when he was in Abilene (Kansas) High School. His football career ended when, as a cadet at West Point, he tackled Jim Thorpe in an Army-Carlisle game and wrenched his knee. Later, he coached football at Peacock Military Academy in San Antonio, Texas, in 1915. At the time, he was a second lieutenant in the Army and was paid $150 extra for his coaching. In 1916, he moved up, coaching at St. Louis College in San Antonio.

John F. Kennedy enjoyed touch football with his family. Richard M. Nixon played football for his alma mater, Whittier College, in California. And Ronald Reagan played guard for his high school, the Dixon (Illinois) Dukes in 1927, and later at Eureka College in Illinois.

The president who came closest to playing in the NFL was Gerald Ford. Ford was the center at the University of Michigan from 1931 to 1934 and was named the team's Most Valuable Player in 1934. In 1935, he played in the College All-Star Game against the Bears. The collegians lost, 5-0, but Ford received $100 for the game, making him a pro for a short time. He also played in the East-West Shrine Game in 1935. The East lost, despite Ford's playing fifty-eight minutes of the sixty-minute game. Both the Lions and the Packers offered him a tryout, but he decided to go to Yale University's law school.

THE HALL OF FAME

The ultimate home for the NFL's superstars is the Pro Football Hall of Fame in Canton, Ohio. It is not too far from the Hupmobile Agency where the league came into being in 1920. It opened on September 7, 1963 as a two-building complex. Today it is a four-building, 51,000-square-foot facility. The address is 2121 George Halas Drive, NW, Canton, Ohio 44708.

Here are the names of the men in the Hall of Fame, beginning with the first class of enshrinees in 1963.

1963

Sammy Baugh — Quarterback, Coach

Bert Bell — NFL Commissioner, Coach, Owner

Johnny Blood (McNally) — Halfback, Coach

Joe Carr — NFL President, Founder, Owner

Dutch Clark — Quarterback, Coach

Red Grange — Halfback

George Halas — End, Coach, Founder, Owner

Mel Hein — Center, Coach, League Official

Pete Henry — Tackle, Coach

Cal Hubbard — Tackle

Don Hutson — End

Curly Lambeau — Halfback, Coach, Founder

Tim Mara — Owner

George Preston Marshall — Owner

Bronko Nagurski — Fullback

Ernie Nevers — Fullback, Tailback, Coach

Jim Thorpe — Halfback, Coach, NFL President

1964

Jimmy Conzelman — Quarterback, Coach, Owner

Ed Healey — Tackle

Clarke Hinkle — Fullback

Mike Michalske — Guard

Art Rooney — Owner

George Trafton — Center

1965

Guy Chamberlain — End, Coach

Paddy Driscoll — Quarterback, Coach

Danny Fortmann — Guard

Otto Graham — Quarterback, Coach

Sid Luckman — Quarterback

Steve Van Buren — Halfback

Bob Waterfield — Quarterback, Kicker, Coach

1966

Bill Dudley — Halfback, Tailback, Kicker

Joe Guyon — Fullback, Tailback

Arnie Herber — Quarterback

Walt Kiesling — Guard, Coach

George McAfee — Halfback

Steve Owen — Tackle, Coach

Shorty Ray — League Official

1967

Chuck Bednarik — Center, Linebacker

Charles Bidwell — Owner

Paul Brown — Coach, Owner

Bobby Layne — Quarterback

Dan Reeves — Owner

Ken Strong — Halfback, Kicker

Joe Stydahar — Tackle, Coach

Emlen Tunnell — Defensive Back

1968

Cliff Battles — Halfback, Tailback, Coach

Art Donovan — Defensive Tackle

Elroy Hirsch — End, General Manager

1968 Continued

Wayne Millner — End, Coach

Marion Motley — Fullback

Charlie Trippi — Halfback, Quarterback

Alex Wojcieshowicz — Center, Linebacker

1969

Turk Edwards — Tackle, Coach

Greasy Neale — Coach, End

Leo Nomellini — Defensive Tackle

Joe Perry — Fullback

Ernie Stautner — Defensive Tackle

1970

Jack Christiansen — Defensive Back, Coach

Tom Fears — End, Coach

Hugh McElhenny — Halfback

Pete Pihos — End

1971

Jim Brown — Fullback

Bill Hewitt — End

Bruiser Kinard — Tackle

Vince Lombardi — Coach

Andy Robustelli — Defensive End, General Manager

Y.A. Tittle — Quarterback

Norm Van Brocklin — Quarterback, Coach

1972

Lamar Hunt — AFL Founder, Owner

Gino Marchetti — Defensive End

Ollie Matson — Halfback

Ace Parker — Tailback, Quarterback

1973

Raymond Berry — End, Coach

Jim Parker — Offensive Tackle, Guard

Joe Schmidt — Linebacker, Coach

1974

Tony Canadeo — Halfback, Fullback

Bill George — Guard, Linebacker, Tackle

Lou Groza — Kicker, Tackle

Dick Lane — Defensive Back

1975

Roosevelt Brown — Offensive Tackle

George Connor — Tackle, Guard, Linebacker

Dante Lavelli — End

Lenny Moore — Halfback, Flanker

1976

Ray Flaherty — End, Coach

Len Ford — End

Jim Taylor — Fullback

1977

Frank Gifford — Halfback, Flanker

Forrest Gregg — Offensive Tackle

Gale Sayers — Halfback

Bart Starr — Quarterback

Bill Willis — Guard

1978

Lance Alworth — Wide Receiver

Weeb Ewbank — Coach

Tuffy Leemans — Fullback

Ray Nitschke — Linebacker

Larry Wilson — Defensive Back

1979

Dick Butkus — Linebacker

Yale Lary — Defensive Back, Punter

Ron Mix — Offensive Tackle

Johnny Unitas — Quarterback

1980

Herb Adderley — Defensive Back

1980 Continued
Deacon Jones — Defensive End
Bob Lilly — Defensive Tackle
Jim Otto — Center
1981
Red Badgro — End
George Blanda — Quarterback, Kicker
Willie Davis — Defensive End
Jim Ringo — Center, Coach
1982
Doug Atkins — Defensive End
Sam Huff — Linebacker
George Musso — Tackle, Guard
Merlin Olsen — Defensive Tackle
1983
Bobby Bell — Linebacker
Sid Gilman — Coach
Sonny Jurgensen — Quarterback
Bobby Mitchell — Halfback, Wide Receiver
Paul Warfield — Wide Receiver
1984
Willie Brown — Defensive Back
Mike McCormack — Tackle
Charley Taylor — Wide Receiver
Arnie Weinmeister — Defensive Tackle
1985
Frank Gatski — Center
Joe Namath — Quarterback
Pete Rozelle — Commissioner
O.J. Simpson — Running Back
Roger Staubach — Quarterback
1986
Paul Hornung — Quarterback, Half-back, Kicker
Ken Houston — Defensive Back
Willie Lanier — Linebacker
Fran Tarkenton — Quarterback
Doak Walker — Halfback, Kicker
1987
Larry Csonka — Fullback
Len Dawson — Quarterback
Joe Greene — Defensive Tackle
John Henry Johnson — Fullback
Jim Langer — Center
Don Maynard — Wide Receiver
Gene Upshaw — Offensive Guard
1988
Fred Biletnikoff — Wide Receiver
Mike Ditka — Tight End, Coach
Jack Ham — Linebacker
Alan Page — Defensive Tackle
1989
Mel Blount — Cornerback
Terry Bradshaw — Quarterback
Art Shell — Offensive Tackle, Coach
Willie Wood — Safety
1990
Buck Buchanan — Defensive Tackle
Bob Griese — Quarterback
Franco Harris — Running Back
Ted Hendricks — Linebacker
Jack Lambert — Linebacker
Tom Landry — Defensive Back, Coach
Bob St. Clair — Offensive Tackle
1991
Earl Campbell — Running Back
John Hannah — Offensive Guard
Stan Jones — Offensive Guard, Defensive Tackle
Tex Schramm — General Manager
Jan Stenerud — Kicker

1992
Lem Barney — Cornerback, Punter, Kick Returner

Al Davis — Owner, Coach
John Mackey — Tight End
John Riggins — Running Back

THE BERT BELL TROPHY

The Bert Bell Memorial Trophy, named after the former NFL commissioner, is awarded to the outstanding NFL rookie by a panel of sports experts.

1964 — Charlie Taylor, Redskins wide receiver

1965 — Gale Sayers, Bears running back

1966 — Tommy Nobis, Falcons linebacker

1967 — Mel Farr, Lions running back

1968 — Earl McCullough, Lions wide receiver

1969 — Calvin Hill, Cowboys running back

1970 — Raymond Chester, Oakland Raiders tight end

1971 — AFC: Jim Plunkett, Patriots quarterback
NFC: John Brockington, Packers running back

1972 — AFC: Franco Harris, Steelers running back
NFC: Willie Buchanan, Packers defensive back

1973 — AFC: Bobbie Clark, Bengals running back
NFC: Chuck Foreman, Vikings running back

1974 — Don Woods, Chargers running back

1975 — AFC: Robert Brazile, Oilers linebacker
NFC: Steve Bartkowski, Falcons quarterback

1976 — AFC: Mike Haynes, Patriots cornerback
NFC: Sammy White, Vikings wide receiver

1977 — Tony Dorsett, Cowboys running back

1978 — Earl Campbell, Oilers running back

1979 — Ottis Anderson, St. Louis Cardinals running back

1980 — Billy Sims, Lions running back

1981 — Lawrence Taylor, Giants linebacker

1982 — Marcus Allen, Raiders running back

1983 — Eric Dickerson, Rams running back

1984 — Louis Lipps, Steelers wide receiver

1985 — Eddie Brown, Bengals wide receiver

1986 — Rueben Mayes, Saints running back

1987 — Bo Jackson, Raiders running back

1988 — John Stephens, Patriots running back

1989 — Barry Sanders, Lions running back

1990 — Eric Green, Steelers tight end

1991 — Mike Croel, Broncos linebacker

THE GEORGE HALAS TROPHY

The George Halas Trophy, named after the former owner-coach of the Chicago Bears, is awarded to the outstanding defensive player in the NFL by a panel of sports experts. 1966 — Larry Wilson, St. Louis Cardinals

1967 — Deacon Jones, Rams
1968 — Deacon Jones, Rams
1969 — Dick Butkus, Bears
1970 — Dick Butkus, Bears
1971 — Carl Eller, Vikings
1972 — Joe Greene, Steelers
1973 — Alan Page, Vikings
1974 — Joe Greene, Steelers
1975 — Curley Culp, Oilers
1976 — Jerry Sherk, Browns
1977 — Harvey Martin, Cowboys
1978 — Randy Gradishar, Broncos
1979 — Lee Roy Selmon, Buccaneers

1980 — Lester Hayes, Oakland Raiders
1981 — Joe Klecko, Jets
1982 — Mark Gastineau, Jets
1983 — Jack Lambert, Steelers
1984 — Mike Haynes, Raiders
1985 — Howie Long, Raiders
Andre Tippett, Patriots
1986 — Lawrence Taylor, Giants
1987 — Reggie White, Eagles
1988 — Mike Singletary, Bears
1989 — Tim Harris, Packers
1990 — Bruce Smith, Bills
1991 — Pat Swilling, Saints

THE JIM THORPE TROPHY

The Jim Thorpe Trophy, named after the all-round athlete who was a player on several early teams and the first president of the league, is awarded to the league's most valuable player and is chosen by the NFL Players Association.

1955 — Harlon Hill, Bears
1956 — Frank Gifford, Giants
1957 — Johnny Unitas, Baltimore Colts
1958 — Jim Brown, Browns
1959 — Charley Conerly, Giants
1960 — Norm Van Brocklin, Eagles
1961 — Y.A. Tittle, Giants
1962 — Jim Taylor, Packers
1963 — Jim Brown, Giants
Y.A. Tittle, Giants
1964 — Lenny Moore, Baltimore Colts
1965 — Jim Brown, Browns
1966 — Bart Starr, Packers

1967 — Johnny Unitas, Baltimore Colts
1968 — Earl Morrall, Baltimore Colts
1969 — Roman Gabriel, Rams
1970 — John Brodie, 49ers
1971 — Bob Griese, Dolphins
1972 — Larry Brown, Redskins
1973 — O.J. Simpson, Bills
1974 — Ken Stabler, Oakland Raiders
1975 — Fran Tarkenton, Vikings
1976 — Bert Jones, Baltimore Colts
1977 — Walter Payton, Bears
1978 — Earl Campbell, Oilers

1979 — Earl Campbell, Oilers
1980 — Earl Campbell, Oilers
1981 — Ken Anderson, Bengals
1982 — Dan Fouts, Chargers
1983 — Joe Theismann, Redskins
1984 — Dan Marino, Dolphins
1985 — Walter Payton, Bears

1986 — Phil Simms, Giants
1987 — Jerry Rice, 49ers
1988 — Roger Craig, 49ers
1989 — Joe Montana, 49ers
1990 — Warren Moon, Oilers
1991 — Thurman Thomas, Bills

SUPER BOWL MOST VALUABLE PLAYERS

1967 — Bart Starr, Packers
1968 — Bart Starr, Packers
1969 — Joe Namath, Jets
1970 — Len Dawson, Chiefs
1971 — Chuck Howley, Cowboys
1972 — Roger Staubach, Cowboys
1973 — Jake Scott, Dolphins
1974 — Larry Csonka, Dolphins
1975 — Franco Harris, Steelers
1976 — Lynn Swann, Steelers
1977 — Fred Biletnikoff, Oakland
Raiders
1978 — Randy White, Cowboys
Harvey Martin, Cowboys
1979 — Terry Bradshaw, Steelers

1980 — Terry Bradshaw, Steelers
1981 — Jim Plunkett, Oakland
Raiders
1982 — Joe Montana, 49ers
1983 — John Riggins, Redskins
1984 — Marcus Allen, Raiders
1985 — Joe Montana, 49ers
1986 — Richard Dent, Bears
1987 — Phil Simms, Giants
1988 — Doug Williams, Redskins
1989 — Jerry Rice, 49ers
1990 — Joe Montana, 49ers
1991 — Ottis Anderson, Giants
1992 — Mark Rypien, Redskins

PLAYER OF THE YEAR

The most valuable player in the NFL has been chosen by various groups over the years. For nine years, the league itself awarded the Joe F. Carr Trophy, named after the second league president (1921-39). It is represented in the following list by (C). The United Press International (UPI) made the award from 1953 to 1969. The Associated Press (AP) has given an award since 1957. The Maxwell Club (M) of Philadelphia has given one since 1959. The Professional Football Writers Association (PFWA) award began in 1976.

1938 — Mel Hein, Giants center (C)
1939 — Parker Hall, Cleveland Rams halfback (C)
1940 — Ace Parker, Brooklyn Dodgers halfback (C)

1941 — Don Hutson, Packers end (C)
1942 — Don Hutson, Packers end (C)
1943 — Sid Luckman, Bears quarterback (C)

1944 — Frank Sinkwich, Lions halfback (C)

1945 — Bob Waterfield, Cleveland Rams quarterback (C)

1946 — Bill Dudley, Steelers halfback (C)

1947-1952 — No MVP chosen

1953 — Otto Graham, Browns quarterback (UPI)

1954 — Joe Perry, 49ers guard (UPI)

1955 — Otto Graham, Browns quarterback (UPI)

1956 — Frank Gifford, Giants halfback (UPI)

1957 — Y.A. Tittle, Giants quarterback (UPI)
Jim Brown, Browns fullback (AP)

1958 — Jim Brown, Browns fullback (UPI)
Gino Marchetti, Baltimore Colts defensive end (AP)

1959 — Johnny Unitas, Baltimore Colts quarterback (UPI, M)
Charley Conerly, Giants quarterback (AP)

1960 — Norm Van Brocklin, Eagles quarterback (UPI, AP [tie], M)
Joe Schmidt, Lions linebacker (AP [tie])

1961 — Paul Hornung, Packers halfback (UPI, AP, M)

1962 — Y.A. Tittle, Giants quarterback (UPI)
Jim Taylor, Packers fullback (AP)
Andy Robustelli, Giants defensive end (M)

1963 — Jim Brown, Browns fullback (UPI, M)
Y.A. Tittle, Giants quarterback (AP)

1964 — Johnny Unitas, Baltimore Colts quarterback (UPI, AP, M)

1965 — Jim Brown, Browns fullback (UPI, AP)
Pete Retzlaff, Eagles tight end (M)

1966 — Bart Starr, Packers quarterback (UPI, AP)
Don Meredith, Cowboys quarterback (M)

1967 — Johnny Unitas, Baltimore quarterback (UPI, AP, M)

1968 — Earl Morrall, Baltimore Colts quarterback (UPI, AP)
Leroy Kelly, Browns running back (M)

1969 — Roman Gabriel, Rams quarterback (UPI, AP, M)

1970 — John Brodie, 49ers quarterback (AP)
George Blanda, Oakland Raiders quarterback kicker (M)

1971 — Alan Page, Vikings defensive tackle (AP)
Roger Staubach, Cowboys quarterback (M)

1972 — Larry Brown, Redskins running back (AP, M)

1973 — O.J. Simpson, Bills running back (AP, M)

1974 — Ken Stabler, Oakland Raiders quarterback (AP)
Merlin Olsen, Rams (M)

1975 — Fran Tarkenton, Vikings quarterback (AP, M)

1976 — Bert Jones, Baltimore Colts quarterback (AP, PFWA) Ken Stabler, Oakland Raiders quarterback (M)

1977 — Walter Payton, Bears running back (AP, PFWA) Bob Griese, Dolphins quarterback (M)

1978 — Terry Bradshaw, Steelers quarterback (AP, M) Earl Campbell, Oilers running back (PFWA)

1979 — Earl Campbell, Oilers running back (AP, M, PFWA)

1980 — Brian Sipe, Browns quarterback (AP, PFWA) Ron Jaworski, Eagles quarterback (M)

1981 — Ken Anderson, Bengals quarterback (AP, M, PFWA)

1982 — Mark Moseley, Redskins kicker (AP) Joe Theismann, Redskins quarterback (M) Dan Fouts, Chargers quarterback (PFWA)

1983 — Joe Theismann, Redskins quarterback (AP, PFWA) John Riggins, Redskins running back (M)

1984 — Dan Marino, Dolphins quarterback (AP, M, PFWA)

1985 — Marcus Allen, Raiders running back (AP, PFWA) Walter Payton, Bears running back (M)

1986 — Lawrence Taylor, Giants linebacker (AP, M, PFWA)

1987 — John Elway, Broncos quarterback (AP) Jerry Rice, 49ers wide receiver (M, PFWA)

1988 — Boomer Esiason, Bengals quarterback (AP, PFWA) Randall Cunningham, Eagles quarterback (M)

1989 — Joe Montana, 49ers quarterback (AP, M, PFWA)

1990 — Randall Cunningham, Eagles quarterback (M, PFWA) Joe Montana, 49ers quarterback (AP)

1991 — Thurman Thomas, Bills halfback (AP, PFWA) Barry Sanders, Lions halfback/fullback (M)

NFC PLAYER OF THE YEAR

This selection has been made by United Press International since 1970. Beginning in 1983, UPI gave two awards — one for offense and one for defense.

1970 — John Brodie, 49ers quarterback

1971 — Alan Page, Vikings defensive tackle

1972 — Larry Brown, Redskins running back

1973 — John Hadl, Rams quarterback

1974 — Jim Hart, St. Louis Cardinals quarterback

1975 — Fran Tarkenton, Vikings quarterback

1976 — Chuck Foreman, Vikings running back

1977 — Walter Payton, Bears running back

1978 — Archie Manning, Saints quarterback

1979 — Ottis Anderson, St. Louis Cardinals running back

1980 — Ron Jaworski, Eagles quarterback

1981 — Tony Dorsett, Cowboys running back

1982 — Mark Moseley, Redskins kicker

1983 — Offense: Eric Dickerson, Rams running back
Defense: Lionel Taylor, Giants linebacker

1984 — Offense: Eric Dickerson, Rams running back
Defense: Mike Singletary, Bears linebacker

1985 — Offense: Walter Payton, Bears running back
Defense: Mike Singletary, Bears linebacker

1986 — Offense: Eric Dickerson, Rams running back
Defense: Lionel Taylor, Giants linebacker

1987 — Offense: Jerry Rice, 49ers wide receiver
Defense: Reggie White, Eagles defensive end

1988 — Offense: Roger Craig, 49ers running back
Defense: Mike Singletary, Bears linebacker

1989 — Offense: Joe Montana, 49ers quarterback
Defense: Keith Millard, Vikings defensive tackle

1990 — Offense: Randall Cunningham, Eagles quarterback
Defense: Charles Haley, 49ers defensive end/linebacker

1991 — Offense: Mark Rypien, Redskins quarterback
Defense: Reggie White, Eagles defensive end/tackle

AFL-AFC PLAYER OF THE YEAR

This selection has been made by United Press International since 1960 to the top player in the AFL (1960-69) and AFC (since 1970). Beginning in 1983, UPI gave two awards — one for offense and one for defense.

1960 — Abner Hayes, Dallas Texans halfback

1961 — George Blanda, Oilers quarterback

1962 — Cookie Gilchrist, Bills fullback

1963 — Lance Alworth, Chargers flanker

1964 — Gino Cappelletti, Boston Patriots flanker/kicker

1965 — Paul Lowe, Chargers halfback

1966 — Jim Nance, Boston Patriots fullback

1967 — Joe Namath, Jets quarterback

1969 — Daryl Lamonica, Oakland Raiders quarterback

1970 — George Blanda, Oakland Raiders quarterback/kicker

1971 — Otis Taylor, Chiefs wide receiver

1972 — O.J. Simpson, Bills running back

1973 — O.J. Simpson, Bills running back

1974 — Ken Stabler, Oakland Raiders quarterback

1975 — O.J. Simpson, Bills running back

1976 — Bert Jones, Baltimore Colts quarterback

1977 — Craig Morton, Broncos quarterback

1978 — Earl Campbell, Oilers running back

1979 — Dan Fouts, Chargers quarterback

1980 — Brian Sipe, Browns quarterback

1981 — Ken Anderson, Bengals quarterback

1982 — Dan Fouts, Chargers quarterback

1983 — Offense: Curt Warner, Seahawks running back
Defense: Rod Martin, Raiders linebacker

1984 — Offense: Dan Marino, Dolphins quarterback

Defense: Mark Gastineau, Jets defensive end

1985 — Offense: Marcus Allen, Raiders running back
Defense: Andre Tippett, Patriots linebacker

1986 — Offense: Curt Warner, Seahawks running back
Defense: Rulon Jones, Broncos defensive end

1987 — Offense: John Elway, Broncos quarterback
Defense: Bruce Smith, Bills defensive end

1988 — Offense: Boomer Esiason, Bengals quarterback
Defense: Bruce Smith, Bills defensive end

1989 — Offense: Christian Okoye, Chiefs running back
Defense: Michael Dean Penny, Browns nose tackle

1990 — Offense: Warren Moon, Oilers quarterback
Defense: Bruce Smith, Bills defensive end

1991 — Offense: Thurman Thomas, Bills halfback
Defense: Cornelius Bennett, Bills linebacker

NUMBER ONE DRAFT CHOICES

The NFL draft of college players began in 1936. The team with the worst record the preceding year gets the first pick, unless it has traded it away. Here are the teams and the college players they chose, along with their schools and positions.

1936 — Eagles: Jay Berwanger, University of Chicago halfback

1937 — Eagles: Sam Francis, University of Nebraska fullback

1938 — Cleveland Rams: Corbett Davis, Indiana University fullback

1939 — Chicago Cardinals: Ki Aldrich, Texas Christian University center

1940 — Chicago Cardinals: George Cafego, University of Tennessee halfback

1941 — Bears: Tom Harmon, University of Michigan halfback

1942 — Steelers: Bill Dudley, University of Virginia halfback

1943 — Lions: Frank Sinkwich, University of Georgia halfback

1944 — Boston Yanks: Angelo Bertelli, University of Notre Dame quarterback

1945 — Chicago Cardinals: Charley Trippi, University of Georgia halfback

1946 — Boston Yanks: Frank Dancewicz, University of Notre Dame quarterback

1947 — Bears: Bob Fenimore, Oklahoma State (now Oklahoma A&M) halfback

1948 — Redskins: Harry Gilmer, University of Alabama quarterback

1949 — Eagles: Chuck Bednarik, University of Pennsylvania center

1950 — Lions: Leon Hart, University of Notre Dame end

1951 — Giants: Kyle Rote, Southern Methodist University halfback

1952 — Rams: Bill Wade, Vanderbilt University quarterback

1953 — 49ers: Harry Babcock, University of Georgia end

1954 — Browns: Bobby Garrett, Stanford University quarterback

1955 — Baltimore Colts: George Shaw, University of Oregon quarterback

1956 — Steelers: Gary Glick, Colorado A&M defensive back

1957 — Packers: Paul Hornung, University of Notre Dame quarterback

1958 — Chicago Cardinals: King Hill, Rice University quarterback

1959 — Packers: Randy Duncan, University of Iowa quarterback

1960 — Rams: Billy Cannon, Louisiana State University halfback

1961 — Vikings: Tommey Mason, Tulane University halfback

1962 — Redskins: Ernie Davis, Syracuse University halfback

1963 — Rams: Terry Baker, Oregon State University quarterback

1964 — 49ers: Dave Parks, Texas Tech end

1965 — Giants: Tucker Frederickson, Auburn University halfback

1966 — Falcons: Tommy Nobis, University of Texas linebacker

1967 — Baltimore Colts: Bubba Smith, Michigan State University defensive tackle

1968 — Vikings: Ron Yary, University of Southern California tackle

1969 — Bills: O.J. Simpson, University of Southern California running back

1970 — Steelers: Terry Bradshaw, Louisiana Tech quarterback

1971 — Patriots: Jim Plunkett, Stanford University quarterback

1972 — Bills: Walt Patulski, University of Notre Dame defensive end

1973 — Oilers: John Matuszak, University of Tampa defensive end

1974 — Cowboys: Ed "Too Tall" Jones, Tennessee State University defensive end

1975 — Falcons: Steve Bartkowski, University of California quarterback

1976 — Buccaneers: LeRoy Selmon, University of Oklahoma defensive end

1977 — Buccaneers: Ricky Bell, University of Southern California running back

1978 — Oilers: Earl Campbell, University of Texas running back

1979 — Bills: Tom Cousineau, Ohio State University linebacker

1980 — Lions: Billy Sims, University of Oklahoma running back

1981 — Saints: George Rogers, University of South Carolina running back

1982 — Patriots: Kenneth Sims, University of Texas defensive tackle

1983 — Baltimore Colts: John Elway, Stanford University quarterback

1984 — Patriots: Irving Fryar, University of Nebraska wide receiver

1985 — Bills: Bruce Smith, Virginia Tech defensive end

1986 — Buccaneers: Bo Jackson, Auburn University running back

1987 — Buccaneers: Vinny Testaverde, University of Miami quarterback

1988 — Falcons: Aundray Bruce, Auburn University linebacker

1989 — Cowboys: Troy Aikman, University of California at Los Angeles quarterback

1990 — Colts: Jeff George, University of Illinois quarterback

1991 — Cowboys: Russell Maryland, University of Miami defensive tackle

1992 — Colts: Steve Emtman, University of Washington defensive tackle

WINNINGEST NFL COACHES

Here, in order of their number of victories, are the top coaches in the history of the NFL. Listed are the coaches, their number of years coaching, their teams, and their won-lost records:

Coaches	Years Coaching	Teams	Won-Lost Record
George Halas	40	Bears	325-151
Don Shula	20	Colts, Dolphins	306-145
Tom Landry	29	Cowboys	270-178
Curly Lambeau	33	Packers, Cardinals, Redskins	229-134
Chuck Noll	23	Steelers	210-155
Chuck Knox	19	Rams, Bills, Seahawks	177-126
Paul Brown	21	Browns, Bengals	170-108
Bug Grant	18	Vikings	168-108
Steve Owen	23	Giants	153-108
Hank Stram	17	Chiefs, Saints	136-100
Weeb Ewbank	20	Colts, Jets	134-130
Sid Gillman	18	Rams, Chargers, Oilers	123-104
George Allen	12	Rams, Redskins	118-54
Joe Gibbs	11	Redskins	131-56
Don Coryell	14	Cardinals, Chargers	114-89
John Madden	10	Raiders	112-39
Buddy Parker	15	Cardinals, Lions, Steelers	107-76
Vince Lombardi	10	Packers, Redskins	105-35
Bill Walsh	10	49ers	102-63
Lou Saban	16	Patriots, Bills, Broncos	97-100

A PARTING THOUGHT

Perhaps all these records and polls do not really tell who the real superstars were. Let's go back in history and investigate the triple crown. Winning the triple crown means that a player led the league in three separate categories *in one season*. It has been won only three times in NFL history, and is not likely ever to be done again, since these days players play on either offense or defense. In 1943, Sammy Baugh of the Redskins did it by leading in passing, punting, and interceptions. Steve Van Buren of the Eagles accomplished the feat in 1945, leading in rushing, scoring, and kickoff returns. Finally, in 1946, Bill Dudley of the Steelers won it in rushing, punt returns, and interceptions. Those days are gone forever.

5
The Champions

Until 1933, the champion of the league was the team with the best won-lost record, although there were some arguments about that, especially since the teams often did not play the same number of league games. Here are the winners for that period.

1919

The Canton (Ohio) Bulldogs won the title after beating the Massillon (Ohio) Tigers in the last game of the season.

1920

The Akron Pros, with their 6-0-3 record, were clearly the class of the league. Besides, they had scored ninety-five points that year and had given up but seven.

1921

This year was a squeaker, with the Chicago Staleys posting a 9-1-1 mark as the Buffalo All-Americans breathed down their necks with a 9-1-2 record.

1922

The Canton Bulldogs were back in first place this year, going 10-0-2 and giving up only fifteen points.

1923

For the second straight year, the Canton Bulldogs went undefeated, posting an 11-0-1 record and giving up only nineteen points.

1924

For the first time, the league season had a definite beginning date and definite ending date. That meant that games could not be scheduled after the end of the season, which had sometimes upset the final standings. The Cleveland Bulldogs finished in first place with a 7-1-1 record.

1925

Chicago won the championship again, but this time it was another Chicago team — the Cardinals. They went 11-2-1, barely beating out the Pottsville (Pennsylvania) Maroons (10-2-0) because they had played more games.

1926

It was the Frankford (Pennsylvania) Yellow Jackets this year, with its 14-1-2 record.

1927

The New York Giants were the runaway champions, finishing 11-1-1. In a distant second place were the Green Bay Packers, at 7-2-1.

1928

The Providence (Rhode Island) Steam Roller won the championship with an 8-1-2 record. In second place, although they won eleven games, were the Frankford (Pennsylvania) Yellow Jackets. They had played five more games than the Steam Roller, but finished with an 11-3-2 record.

1929

The Green Bay Packers (12-0-1) sneaked past the New York Giants (13-1-1).

1930

For the second straight year, the Green Bay Packers (10-3-1) edged out the New York Giants (13-4-0).

1931

The Green Bay Packers made it three in a row by posting a 12-2-0 record. They nosed out the Portsmouth (Ohio) Spartans, with their 11-3-0 mark.

1932

As had been true since the league began, ties did not count in the standings. At the end of the season, the Chicago Bears (6-1-6) and the Portsmouth (Ohio) Spartans (6-1-4) were tied. In the league's first play-off game, the Bears beat the Spartans 9-0, winning the championship.

THE CHAMPIONSHIP GAMES

Beginning in 1933, with the NFL divided into Eastern and Western divisions, the league decided to schedule a championship game between the winners of the two.

1933

The Western champion Chicago Bears (10-2-1) beat the Eastern champion New York Giants (11-3-0) by a score of 23-21.

1934

The New York Giants (8-5-0) beat the Chicago Bears (13-0-0) by a score of 30-13 in the historic "Sneaker Game." (See Chapter 12.)

1935

It was the Detroit Lions (7-3-2) against the New York Giants (9-3-0) on a muddy field and in a freezing rain and biting wind. Only 15,000 fans showed up to see Detroit win 26-7.

1936

The game this year was an oddity. It was scheduled to be played in the home stadium of the Eastern winner. But Boston Redskins (7-5-0) fans had not shown up in great numbers during the season, and owner George Preston

Marshall got the game moved to New York. The Green Bay Packers (10-1-1) won the game 21-6, and the next year the Redskins were in Washington, D.C.

1937

The Washington Redskins (8-3-0) beat the Chicago Bears (9-1-1) by a score of 28-21.

1938

The New York Giants (8-2-1) beat the Green Bay Packers (8-3-0) by a score of 23-17.

1939

The Green Bay Packers (9-2-0) got their revenge by beating the New York Giants (9-1-1) by a score of 27-0.

1940

The Chicago Bears (8-3-0) beat the Washington Redskins (9-2-0) in the historic 73-0 game. (See Chapter 14.)

1941

Played just two weeks after the Japanese attack on Pearl Harbor, the game ended with the Chicago Bears (10-1-0) beating the New York Giants (8-3-0) by a score of 39-7.

1942

The Washington Redskins (10-1-0) won a bit of revenge for their 1940 pasting by beating the Chicago Bears (11-0-0), 14-6.

1943

It was the Chicago Bears (8-1-1) against the Washington Redskins (6-3-1) once again, and this time the Bears won the game 41-21.

1944

It was the Green Bay Packers (8-2-0) again, this time playing the New York Giants (8-1-1) and winning 14-7.

1945

In a kicking game, the Cleveland Rams (9-1-0) beat the Washington Redskins (8-2-0) by a score of 15-14.

1946

The game was tied going into the fourth quarter, but the Chicago Bears (8-2-1) scored ten points and beat the New York Giants (7-3-1), 24-14.

1947

It was the first appearance of the Chicago Cardinals (9-3-0) in the championship game, and they beat the Philadelphia Eagles (8-4-0) by a score of 28-21.

1948

The Chicago Cardinals (11-1-0) were back in the championship game. This time it was in a blizzard. They faced the Philadelphia Eagles (9-2-1) and lost in the final quarter, 7-0.

1949
The Rams (8-2-2) were now in Los Angeles, having moved from Cleveland in 1946, and they faced the Philadelphia Eagles (11-1-0). But they lost in a drenching rain, 14-0.

1950
In its first year, a brand-new team, the Cleveland Browns (10-2-0), beat the Los Angeles Rams (9-3-0) by a score of 30-28.

1951
It was the Cleveland Browns (11-1-1) again against the Los Angeles Rams (8-4-0). But this time the Rams won, 24-17.

1952
The Detroit Lions (9-3-0) tied the Los Angeles Rams (also 9-3-0) in the regular season, but beat them in a special play-off game, 31-21. The Lions went on to beat the Cleveland Browns, 17-7, for the championship.

1953
The game was close all the way, with the Detroit Lions (10-2-0) beating the Cleveland Browns (11-1-0) 17-16 in the last two and one-half minutes.

1954
The Cleveland Browns (9-3-0) gained sweet revenge over the Detroit Lions (9-2-1) by humiliating them 56-10.

1955
The Cleveland Browns (9-2-1) were back again — this time playing the Los Angeles Rams (8-3-1). It was another rout for the Browns; this time they won 38-14.

1956
The old rivals, the Chicago Bears (9-2-1) and the New York Giants (8-3-1), were at it again this year. The Giants won easily, 47-7.

1957
The Detroit Lions (8-4-0) ended the season tied with the San Francisco 49ers but beat them 59-14 in a play-off game. They went on to humiliate the Cleveland Browns (9-2-1) in the championship game, by a score of 59-14.

1958
The New York Giants (9-3-0) faced the Baltimore Colts (9-3-0) in a game that would go to the league's first sudden death overtime. After eight minutes, fifteen seconds of the extra period, the Colts scored a touchdown (no PAT was attempted) to win 23-17.

1959
It was the Baltimore Colts (9-3-0) against the New York Giants (10-2-0) again. And the Colts did it again, winning 31-16.

1960
It was a close game most of the way as the Philadelphia Eagles (10-2-0) beat the Green Bay Packers (8-4-0), 17-13.

1961
The Green Bay Packers (11-3-0) were back. And this time they won — beating the New York Giants (10-3-1) by a score of 37-0.

1962
Once again it was the Green Bay Packers (13-1-0) against the New York Giants (12-2-0). And the Packers did it again, 16-7, on a rock-hard frozen field with winds gusting to forty miles per hour.

1963
The New York Giants (11-3-0) were back again this year, but this time they faced the Chicago Bears (11-1-2). And they lost again, 14-10.

1964
The Cleveland Browns (10-3-1) and the Baltimore Colts (12-2-0) were back in the championship game. This time, Cleveland engineered a rout, 27-0.

1965
When the Green Bay Packers (10-3-1) ended the season tied with the Baltimore Colts, the play-off game was perhaps more exciting than the championship game. It ended in the thirteenth minute of overtime with a field goal, and the Packers won 13-10. They went on to beat the Cleveland Browns (11-3-0) by a score of 23-12.

THE SUPER BOWL ARRIVES

With the consolidation of the National Football League and the American Football League, it was decided that the winners of each league would play each other in a championship game, which was later to become known as the Super Bowl.

These games were to be held in January following the regular season's end and after the various play-offs had been played to determine the two champions.

1966 — Super Bowl I
The Green Bay Packers (12-2-0) beat the Dallas Cowboys (10-3-1) 34-27 for the NFL championship, while in the AFL, the Kansas City Chiefs (11-2-1) beat the Buffalo Bills (9-4-1) 31-7. In the Super Bowl, Green Bay beat the Chiefs, 35-10.

1967 — Super Bowl II
The Green Bay Packers (9-4-1) beat the Dallas Cowboys (9-5-0) again in the NFL, 21-17. In the AFL, it was the Oakland Raiders (13-1-0) beating the Houston Oilers (9-4-1) by a score of 40-7. In the Super Bowl, the Packers beat the Raiders, 33-14.

1968 — Super Bowl III
In the NFL, it was the Baltimore Colts (13-1-0) beating the Cleveland Browns (10-4-0), 34-0. In the AFL, the New York Jets (11-3-0) beat the

Oakland Raiders (12-2-0), 27-23. The Jets won the Super Bowl, 16-7, in the championship that quarterback Joe Namath had "guaranteed." (See Chapter 12.)

1969 — Super Bowl IV

The NFL championship was won by the Minnesota Vikings (12-2-0) when they beat the Cleveland Browns (10-3-1), 27-7. In the AFL, the title was won by the Kansas City Chiefs (11-3-0) when they beat the Oakland Raiders (12-1-1), 17-7. In the Super Bowl, the Chiefs handled the Vikings, 23-7.

1970 — Super Bowl V

This year the NFL was divided into two conferences — the National and the American. In the NFC, the Dallas Cowboys (10-4-0) beat the San Francisco 49ers (10-3-1), 17-10. The AFC was won by the Baltimore Colts (11-2-1) when they beat the Oakland Raiders (8-4-2), 27-17. The Super Bowl was won by Baltimore in a squeaker, 16-13.

1971 — Super Bowl VI

In the NFC, the Dallas Cowboys (11-3-0) beat the San Francisco 49ers (9-5-0), 14-3. In the AFC, it was the Miami Dolphins (10-3-1) beating the Baltimore Colts (10-4-0) by a score of 21-0 — the first time in ninety-seven games that the Colts had not been able to score. The Super Bowl was won by the Cowboys, with a score of 24-3.

1972 — Super Bowl VII

The NFC was won by the Washington Redskins (11-3-0) when they beat the Dallas Cowboys (10-4-0), 26-3. In the AFC, it was the Miami Dolphins (14-0-0) triumphing over the Pittsburgh Steelers (11-3-0) by 21-17. The Super Bowl was won by the Dolphins, 14-7.

1973 — Super Bowl VIII

The Minnesota Vikings (12-2-0) were NFC champions after beating the Dallas Cowboys (10-4-0) 27-10. In the AFC, the Miami Dolphins (12-2-0) beat the Oakland Raiders (9-4-1) by a score of 27-10. The Super Bowl was won by the Dolphins, 24-7.

1974 — Super Bowl IX

The Minnesota Vikings (10-4-0) were again the NFC champions, beating the Los Angeles Rams (10-4-0), 14-10. In the AFC, it was the Pittsburgh Steelers (10-3-1) over the Oakland Raiders (12-2-0) by a score of 24-13. The Super Bowl was won by the Steelers, 16-6.

1975 — Super Bowl X

In the NFC, the Dallas Cowboys (10-4-0) were back, beating the Los Angeles Rams (12-2-0), 37-7. The AFC was won by the Pittsburgh Steelers (12-2-0) when they beat the Oakland Raiders (11-3-0), 16-10. The Steelers went on to win their second straight Super Bowl, with a score of 21-17.

1976 — Super Bowl XI

The NFC was won by the Minnesota Vikings (11-2-1), beating the Los Angeles Rams (10-3-1), 24-13. The AFC champions were the Oakland Raiders (13-1-0), who beat the Pittsburgh Steelers (10-4-0) by a score of 24-7. The Super Bowl champions were the Raiders, 32-14.

1977 — Super Bowl XII

The NFC champions were the Dallas Cowboys (12-2-0), beating the Minnesota Vikings (9-5-0), 23-6. In the AFC, the Denver Broncos (12-2-0) were the victors over the Oakland Raiders (11-3-0) by a score of 20-17. The Super Bowl was won by Dallas, 27-10.

1978 — Super Bowl XIII

In the NFC, the Dallas Cowboys (12-4-0) beat the Los Angeles Rams (12-4-0) by a score of 28-0. They scored all their points in the second half. The Pittsburgh Steelers (14-2-0) also won big, beating the Houston Oilers (10-6-0) to win the AFC, 34-5. In the championship match between two former Super Bowl champions, the Steelers edged out the Cowboys, 35-31.

1979 — Super Bowl XIV

The Los Angeles Rams (9-7-0) beat the Tampa Bay Buccaneers (10-6-0) 9-0 to win the NFC. The Pittsburgh Steelers (12-4-0) were back again, defeating the Houston Oilers (11-5-0) by a score of 27-13 to win the AFC. Once again, the Steelers took the Super Bowl — this time by a score of 31-19.

1980 — Super Bowl XV

The Philadelphia Eagles (12-4-0) took the NFC when they beat the Dallas Cowboys (12-4-0), 20-7. In the AFC, the winner was the Oakland Raiders (11-5-0), who triumphed over the San Diego Chargers (11-5-0), 34-27. Super Bowl XV was won by the Raiders, with a score of 27-10.

1981 — Super Bowl XVI

In the NFC, it was the San Francisco 49ers (13-3-0) over the Dallas Cowboys (12-4-0) in a squeaker, 28-27. The AFC championship was taken by the Cincinnati Bengals (12-4-0), who beat the San Diego Chargers (10-6-0), 27-7. San Francisco won its first Super Bowl, with a score of 26-21.

1982 — Super Bowl XVII

The Washington Redskins (8-1-0) won the NFC by beating the Dallas Cowboys (6-3-0) 31-17 in this year of the players' strike. In the AFC, it was the Miami Dolphins (7-2-0) over the New York Jets (6-3-0), 14-0. The Redskins handled the Dolphins in the championship game, 27-17.

1983 — Super Bowl XVIII

The Washington Redskins (14-2-0) were back again, defeating the San Francisco 49ers (10-6-0) 24-21 for the NFC title. The Los Angeles Raiders (12-4-0) took the AFC, beating the Seattle Seahawks (9-7-0), 31-14. The Super Bowl was won, 38-9, by the Redskins.

1984 — Super Bowl XIX

In the NFC, the champions were the San Francisco 49ers (15-1-0), who beat the Chicago Bears (10-6-0), 23-0. The AFC was won by the Miami Dolphins (14-2-0), triumphing over the Pittsburgh Steelers (9-7-0) by a score of 45-28. The 49ers took the Super Bowl, 38-16.

1985 — Super Bowl XX

The Chicago Bears (15-1-0) beat the Los Angeles Rams (11-5-0) 24-0 to take the NFC. In the AFC, it was the New England Patriots (11-5-0) over the Miami Dolphins (12-4-0), 31-14. The Bears scored big in the Super Bowl to win 46-10.

1986 — Super Bowl XXI

It was the New York Giants (14-2-0) who won the NFC, beating the Washington Redskins (12-4-0) by a score of 17-0. The Denver Broncos (11-5-0) beat the Cleveland Browns (12-4-0) 23-20 to take the AFC. The championship game saw the Giants winning, 39-20.

1987 — Super Bowl XXII

In the NFC, the Washington Redskins (11-4-0) beat the Minnesota Vikings (8-7-0) 17-10 to take the championship. The winner in the AFC was the Denver Broncos (10-4-1), who outscored the Cleveland Browns (10-5-0), 38-33. The Super Bowl was won by the Redskins, 42-10.

1988 — Super Bowl XXIII

The San Francisco 49ers (10-6-0) beat the Chicago Bears (12-4-0) 28-3 to win the NFC. In the AFC, it was the Cincinnati Bengals (12-4-0) who beat the Buffalo Bills (12-4-0), 21-10. The Super Bowl winner was the 49ers, 20-15.

1989 — Super Bowl XXIV

The NFC champions were the San Francisco 49ers (14-2-0) who beat the Los Angeles Rams (11-5-0) by a score of 30-3. In the AFC, it was the Denver Broncos (11-5-0) over the Cleveland Browns (9-6-1), 37-21. The 49ers won another Super Bowl, this time by a score of 55-10.

1990 — Super Bowl XXV

In the NFC, the New York Giants (13-3-0) took the title by easing past the San Francisco 49ers (14-2-0), 15-13. The Buffalo Bills (13-3-0) won the AFC over the Los Angeles Raiders (12-4-0), 51-3. The Super Bowl went down to the wire, with the Giants winning, 20-19.

1991 — Super Bowl XXVI

The NFC champions were the Washington Redskins (14-2-0), who beat the Detroit Lions (12-4-0), 10-7. In the AFC, the winner was the Buffalo Bills (13-3-0) over the Denver Broncos (12-4-0), 10-7. Washington won the Super Bowl 37-24, in a game that was not as close as the score would indicate.

THE PRO BOWL

The Pro Bowl is an annual post-season exhibition game. It began in 1939 with the championship New York Giants playing a team of professional all-stars. The game continued this way until after the 1942 contest, when it was suspended. It was revived in 1951 under a new format, matching the all-stars of the old National Conference and the American Conference. Until 1962, the game was played by all-stars of the East and West of the NFL. Then, in 1962, another new format was inaugurated with two separate all-star games — one in the NFL and one in the AFL. Finally, in 1971, came the single game as we know it, pitting all-star teams from the AFC and the NFC. Here are the scores.

1939 — New York Giants 13, Pro All-Stars 10

1940 — Green Bay Packers 16, NFL All-Stars 7

1941 — (played in December 1940) Chicago Bears 28, NFL All-Stars 14

1942 — Chicago Bears 35, NFL All-Stars 24

1943 — (played in December 1942) NFL All-Stars 17, Washington Redskins 14

1951 — American Conference 28, National Conference 27

1952 — National Conference 30, American Conference 13

1953 — National Conference 27, American Conference 7

1954 — East 20, West 9

1955 — West 26, East 19

1956 — East 31, West 30

1957 — West 19, East 10

1958 — West 26, East 7

1959 — East 28, West 21

1960 — West 38, East 21

1961 — West 35, East 31

1962 — AFL West 47, AFL East 27
NFL West 31, NFL East 30

1963 — AFL West 21, AFL East 14
NFL East 30, NFL West 20

1964 — AFL West 27, AFL East 24
NFL West 31, NFL East 17

1965 — AFL West 38, AFL East 14
NFL West 34, NFL East 14

1966 — AFL All-Stars 30, Buffalo Bills 19
NFL East 36, NFL West 7

1967 — AFL East 30, AFL West 23
NFL East 20, NFL West 10

1968 — AFL East 25, AFL West 24
NFL West 38, NFL East 20

1969 — AFL West 38, AFL East 25
NFL West 10, NFL East 7

1970 — AFL West 26, AFL East 3
NFL West 16, NFL East 13

1971 — NFC 27, AFC 6

1972 — AFC 26, NFC 13

1973 — AFC 33, NFC 28

1974 — AFC 15, NFC 13

1975 — NFC 17, AFC 10

1976 — NFC 23, AFC 20

1977 — AFC 24, NFC 14

1978 — NFC 14, AFC 13

1979 — NFC 13, AFC 7

1980 — NFC 37, AFC 27

1981 — NFC 21, AFC 7

1982 — AFC 16, NFC 13

1983 — NFC 20, AFC 19

1984 — NFC 45, AFC 3

1985 — AFC 22, NFC 14
1986 — NFC 28, AFC 24
1987 — AFC 10, NFC 6
1988 — AFC 15, NFC 6

1989 — NFC 34, AFC 3
1990 — NFC 27, AFC 21
1991 — AFC 23, NFC 21
1992 — NFC 21, AFC 15

THE COLLEGE ALL-STAR GAME

In 1934, the first College All-Star Game was held at Soldier Field, Chicago. Played before the NFL season started, it pitted the NFL champion team from the previous year against a team of college all-stars from the previous year. Conceived as a charity game, it lasted many years and raised a large amount of money for *Chicago Tribune* Charities. The series ended after the 1976 game for two main reasons. The NFL had won twelve games in a row and eighteen of the last twenty-one, and there was a problem in that the college men often had their preseason training camps with the pros interrupted. Here are the results of the game.

1934 — Chicago Bears 0, All-Stars 0
1935 — Chicago Bears 5, All-Stars 0
1936 — Detroit Lions 7, All-Stars 7
1937 — All-Stars 6, Green Bay Packers 0
1938 — All-Stars 28, Washington Redskins 16
1939 — New York Giants 9, All-Stars 0
1940 — Green Bay Packers 45, All-Stars 28
1941 — Chicago Bears 37, All-Stars 13
1942 — Chicago Bears 21, All-Stars 0
1943 — All-Stars 27, Washington Redskins 7
1944 — Chicago Bears 24, All-Stars 21
1945 — Green Bay Packers 19, All-Stars 7
1946 — All-Stars 16, Los Angeles Rams 0
1947 — All-Stars 16, Chicago Bears 0
1948 — Chicago Cardinals 28, All-Stars 0
1949 — Philadelphia Eagles 38, All-Stars 0
1950 — All-Stars 17, Philadelphia Eagles 7
1951 — Cleveland Browns 33, All-Stars 0
1952 — Los Angeles Rams 10, All-Stars 7
1953 — Detroit Lions 24, All-Stars 10
1954 — Detroit Lions 31, All-Stars 6
1955 — All-Stars 30, Cleveland Browns 27
1956 — Cleveland Browns 26, All-Stars 0

1957 — New York Giants 22, All-Stars 12
1958 — All-Stars 35, Detroit Lions 19
1959 — Baltimore Colts 29, All-Stars 0
1960 — Baltimore Colts 32, All-Stars 7
1961 — Philadelphia Eagles 28, All-Stars 14
1962 — Green Bay Packers 42, All-Stars 20
1963 — All-Stars 20, Green Bay Packers 17
1964 — Chicago Bears 28, All-Stars 17
1965 — Cleveland Browns 24, All-Stars 16
1966 — Green Bay Packers 38, All-Stars 0
1967 — Green Bay Packers 27, All-Stars 0
1968 — Green Bay Packers 34, All-Stars 17
1969 — New York Jets 26, All-Stars 24
1970 — Kansas City Chiefs 24, All-Stars 3
1971 — Baltimore Colts 24, All-Stars 17
1972 — Dallas Cowboys 20, All-Stars 7
1973 — Miami Dolphins 14, All-Stars 3
1974 — Canceled because of the NFL players' strike
1975 — Pittsburgh Steelers 21, All-Stars 14
1976 — Pittsburgh Steelers 24, All-Stars 0

6
Firsts and Lasts

Everything has a beginning and an end. Here are some of the major appearances and disappearances in the world of professional football.

FIRSTS

1902

The Philadelphia Athletics were organized by baseball owner Connie Mack as a companion team for his baseball team of the same name. Using baseball pitcher Rube Waddell in the lineup, they played the first night professional football game. The very first floodlit game had been played on September 29, 1892 in Mansfield, Pennsylvania, between Mansfield College and Wyoming Seminary.

1920

The first professional football rule to be broken occurred when the Akron (Ohio) Pros played to a scoreless tie with the Decatur (Illinois) Staleys. Staleys' coach George Halas had used a player who was under contract to the Chicago Cardinals — Paddy Driscoll.

This being the first year of the new league, season records were set in every category. Here are some of them.

Scoring — Frank Bacon, Dayton (Ohio) Triangles, 32 points

Rushing — Pat Smith, Buffalo (New York) All-Americans, 4 touchdowns

Passing — Al Mahrt, Dayton (Ohio) Triangles, 7 touchdowns

Receiving — (tie) Norb Sacksteder, Dayton (Ohio) Triangles; Dave Reese, Dayton (Ohio) Triangles, 3 touchdowns

Field Goals — (tie) Jim Thorpe, Canton (Ohio) Bulldogs; Jim Laird, Rochester (New York) Jeffersons, 3

Extra Points — (tie) Charlie Copley, Akron (Ohio) Pros; George Kinderdine, Dayton (Ohio) Triangles, 12

1922

The first player deal happened when the Bears bought tackle Ed Healey's contract from the Rock Island (Illinois) Independents for $100.

1929

The first out-of-town preseason training camp was set up by the Chicago Cardinals in Coldwater, Michigan.

The first NFL night game was played on November 6th between the Providence (Rhode Island) Steam Roller and the Chicago Cardinals. It was played in Providence's Kinsley Park, the Cardinals won, 16-0, and the ball was white.

1930
The first indoor professional football game was held in Chicago Stadium between the two Chicago teams—the Bears and the Cardinals. The Bears won, playing on an eighty-yard-long field. The game receipts benefited local unemployed people.

1931
At the end of the season, the first All-Pro team was selected, with the following players being honored.

E: Lavie Dilweg, Green Bay Packers
E: Red Badgro, New York Giants
T: Cal Hubbard, Green Bay Packers
T: George Christensen, Portsmouth (Ohio) Spartans
G: Mike Michalske, Green Bay Packers
G: Butch Gibson, New York Giants
C: Frank McNally, Chicago Cardinals
QB: Dutch Clark, Portsmouth (Ohio) Spartans
HB: Red Grange, Chicago Bears
HB: Johnny Blood (McNally), Green Bay Packers
FB: Ernie Nevers, Chicago Cardinals

1932
The Chicago Bears won the first play-off game to decide the league championship, beating the Portsmouth (Ohio) Spartans, 9-0.

1933
For the first time, official league statistics were kept.
For the first time, the NFL was split into divisions:

Eastern Division	Western Division
Boston Redskins	Chicago Bears
Brooklyn Dodgers	Chicago Cardinals
New York Giants	Cincinnati Reds
Philadelphia Eagles	Green Bay Packers
Pittsburgh Pirates	Portsmouth (Ohio) Spartans

Because of the division, the first championship game between the two winners was held, with the Chicago Bears beating the New York Giants, 23-21.

1934
The first College All-Star Game was held at Chicago's Soldier Field, with the Chicago Bears playing to a 0-0 tie against the All-Stars. Here is the lineup for the Bears and the Collegians.

Position	Bears	All-Stars
E	Bill Hewett	Eggs Manske (Northwestern)
E	Luke Johnsos	Joe Skladany (Pittsburgh)
T	Link Lyman	Moose Kraus (Notre Dame)
T	George Musso	Abe Schwammen (Oregon State)
G	Zuck Carlson	Frank Walton (Pittsburgh)
G	Joe Zeller	Bob Jones (Indiana)
C	Ookie Miller	Chuck Bernard (Michigan)
QB	Carl Brumbaugh	Homer Griffith (Southern California)
HB	Gene Ronzani	Beattie Feathers (Tennessee)
HB	George Corbett	Joe Laws (Iowa)
FB	Bronko Nagurski	Mike Mikulak (Oregon)

The coaches were George Halas of the Bears and Nobel Kizer of Purdue. The game drew 79,432 fans.

The first Thanksgiving Day Football game, starring the Detroit Lions, was held.

The first national radio broadcast of an NFL game was played by the Chicago Bears and the Detroit Lions. It was aired by the Columbia Broadcasting System.

The first undefeated, untied team in history was the Chicago Bears, but they lost the championship game to the New York Giants. (See Chapter 12.)

The first running back to gain at least 1,000 yards in a season was Beattie Feathers of the Chicago Bears — 1,004 yards.

1935

The first pro football cards were printed.

1936

The first college draft was held, and the first draft pick was Jay Berwanger, the Heisman Trophy winner in 1935. He was chosen by the Philadelphia Eagles, who traded his rights to the Chicago Bears, but he wouldn't sign.

Arnie Herber of the Green Bay Packers became the first player to pass for more than 1,000 yards in a season. His mark was 1,239 yards.

1937

The first team band was formed by the Washington Redskins.

1938

The first player in the modern era to wear a moustache was Ace Parker of the Brooklyn Dodgers.

1939

The first NFL game to be televised was the October 22nd game between the Brooklyn Dodgers and the Philadelphia Eagles, at Ebbetts Field in Brooklyn. The Dodgers won 23-14. This was not the first ever televised football game, however. In September of that year, Fordham University had played Waynesburg College on Randall's Island, New York, and the game was aired on station W2XBS.

Parker Hall of the Cleveland Rams was the first to complete more than 100 passes in a season. His mark was 106.

For the first time, the total league attendance passed one million fans.

The first Pro Bowl was played at Wrigley Field in Los Angeles before about 20,000 fans. The New York Giants beat a team of professional all-star football players, 13-10. Here are the two lineups.

Position	Giants	All-Stars
E	Jim Lee Howell	Gaynell Tinsley (Chicago Cardinals)
E	Jim Poole	Perry Schwartz (Brooklyn Dodgers)
T	Ed Widseth	Joe Stydahar (Chicago Bears)
T	Ox Parry	Bruiser Kinard (Brooklyn Dodgers)
G	Orville Tuttle	Byron Gentry (Pittsburgh Pirates)
G	Kayo Lunday	Pete Mehringer (Canton Bulldogs)
C	Mel Hein	John Wiatrak (Detroit Lions)
QB	Nello Falaschi	Ernie Pinckert (Washington Redskins)
HB	Ward Cuff	Sammy Baugh (Washington Redskins)
FB	Ed Danowski	Clarke Hinkle (Green Bay Packers)

The coaches were Steve Owen of the New York Giants, and Ray Flaherty (Washington Redskins) and Gus Henderson (Detroit Lions) of the All-Stars.

1940

In the first NFL championship game to be carried on network radio, the Chicago Bears beat the Washington Redskins, 73-0. Red Barber did the play-by-play for 120 radio stations of the Mutual Broadcasting System. (See Chapter 12.)

1941

The first division play-off game was held because the Chicago Bears and Green Bay Packers each finished their seasons at 10-1 and were tied for the title. The Bears won the Western Division championship, 33-14.

1943

The first quarterback to pass for over 400 yards and rack up seven touchdowns in one game was Sid Luckman of the Chicago Bears.

1947

The first quarterback to complete more than 200 passes in one season (210) and gain more than 2,000 yards passing (2,938) was Sammy Baugh of the Washington Redskins.

The first design to appear on the NFL helmet was seen on the headgear of the Los Angeles Rams. Rams halfback Fred Gehrke had painted on rams' horns.

1950

The Los Angeles Rams were the first team to televise all their games, at home and away.

1953

The first black quarterback in modern NFL history played for the Chicago Bears — Willie Thrower.

1956

The Columbia Broadcasting System was the first network to televise regular season games.

For the first time, a radio receiver was installed in a quarterback's helmet to receive play calls from the coach. The coach was the Cleveland Browns' Paul Brown, and the idea was soon outlawed by Commissioner Bert Bell.

1958

For the first time, the average paid attendance (for seventy-two games) topped 40,000 per game (41,752).

For the first time, the total league attendance (for seventy-two games) topped three million fans (3,006,124).

The first sudden death championship game was played, with the Baltimore Colts beating the New York Giants, 23-17.

1960

The first professional football team to issue stock to the public was the Boston Patriots.

The first two passers to gain more than 3,000 yards in a season were Johnny Unitas of the Baltimore Colts (3,099) and Jack Kemp of the Los Angeles Chargers (3,018).

1961

For the first time, the NFL had a single-game million-dollar gate — the title game between the New York Giants and the Green Bay Packers.

1963

The first black assistant coach was hired — Emlen Tunnell of the New York Giants.

1964

The first soccer-style kicker in the NFL appeared with the Buffalo Bills — Pete Gogolak.

1965

The first black official was hired — field judge Burl Tolar.

1966

Lyndon Johnson was the first president to attend an NFL game while in office. He sat in the Washington Redskins owner's box to watch the Redskins play the Baltimore Colts in an exhibition game on August 3rd. Johnson ate two hot dogs, one hamburger, and ice cream, and drank a container of milk. At the same game, Robert and Edward Kennedy were in the Colts' owner's box.

The first nationally televised NFL Monday night game was covered by the Columbia Broadcasting Company.

1967

The first touchdown of an interleague championship game (in what was to be called the Super Bowl) was scored by end Max McGee of the Green Bay Packers. The final score was Packers 35, Kansas City Chiefs 10.

The first quarterback to pass for more than 4,000 yards in one season was Joe Namath of the New York Jets (4,007 yards).

1968

The first coach in the Canadian League to join the NFL was Bud Grant. He moved from the Winnipeg Blue Bombers to the Minnesota Vikings.

The first team to play on an artificial surface was the Houston Oilers, in the Astrodome.

For the first time, the interleague championship game was called the Super Bowl.

The first three-million-dollar gate was taken in at the Super Bowl.

1970

The first defensive player to receive the Most Valuable Player Award in the Super Bowl was Chuck Howley, the Dallas Cowboys linebacker.

1971

The first lineman named most valuable player in the NFL was Alan Page, the Minnesota Vikings tackle.

The first modern Pro Bowl was played with stars from each conference.

1972

The first stock payment by the publicly held New England Patriots was fifteen cents a share.

For the first time in history, ten backs rushed for 1,000 or more yards in a season. They were:

O.J. Simpson of the Buffalo Bills — 1,251 yards

Larry Brown of the Washington Redskins — 1,216 yards

Ron Johnson of the New York Giants — 1,182 yards

Larry Csonka of the Miami Dolphins — 1,117 yards

Marv Hubbard of the Oakland Raiders — 1,100 yards

Franco Harris of the Pittsburgh Steelers — 1,055 yards

Calvin Hill of the Dallas Cowboys — 1,036 yards

Mike Garrett of the San Diego Chargers — 1,031 yards

John Brokington of the Green Bay Packers — 1,027 yards

Jim Kiick of the Miami Dolphins — 1,000 yards

1973

The first player to rush for more than 2,000 yards in a season was O.J. Simpson of the Buffalo Bills. He averaged six yards per carry.

When Ted Fritch, Jr., the center for the Atlanta Falcons, had his name on an NFL card, he became part of the first father-son combination to be so honored. His father, Ted Fritch, Sr., the Green Bay Packers back, had had his card first issued in 1948.

1974

The first regular-season overtime game was played by the Pittsburgh Steelers and the Denver Broncos.

1975

The first player in NFL history to score 2,000 points was George Blanda, the quarterback-kicker of the Oakland Raiders.

For the first time, the "home field advantage" was used in the play-off games, allowing the teams with the best records to host their postseason games.

1976

The first NFL game to be played on a different continent was an exhibition game in Tokyo, Japan, between the St. Louis Cardinals and the San Diego Chargers. The Cardinals won, 20-10.

The first NFL team to lose all of its fourteen games was the Tampa Bay Buccaneers.

1977

The first quarterback to wear glasses in a game was Bob Griese of the Miami Dolphins.

1978

The first player from the American Football League to be elected to the Hall of Fame was Lance Alworth, the end for the San Diego Chargers and the Dallas Cowboys.

1979

On the death of her husband, Georgia Frontiere Rosenbloom became the owner of the Los Angeles Rams — the first woman to hold such a post in the NFL.

1980

The first wild card team to win the Super Bowl was the Oakland Raiders when they beat the Philadelphia Eagles, 27-10.

1986

The first NFL game played in Europe was an exhibition game played at Wembley Stadium in London, England, between the Chicago Bears and the Dallas Cowboys.

1988

The first black quarterback to start a Super Bowl game was Doug

Williams of the Washington Redskins. The first black referee in the league was Johnny Grier.

1989

The first black head coach in the NFL was Art Shell of the Los Angeles Raiders.

1991

When David Shula was named to be the head coach of the Cincinnati Bengals, he joined his father, Don Shula of the Miami Dolphins, as the first father-son combination coaching in the NFL at the same time.

LASTS

1928

The last player to lead the NFL in both rushing and passing touchdowns was Bennie Friedman, the quarterback of the Detroit Wolverines.

1931

The last player to wear neither a helmet nor shoulder pads was Al Nesser, the Cleveland Indians guard.

1933

The last NFL team to be owned by the players was the Brooklyn Dodgers.

1937

The last drop-kicked field goal was scored by Dutch Clark, the Detroit Lions quarterback.

1940

The last player to play without a helmet was Dick Plasman, an end for the Chicago Bears.

1941

The last drop-kicked point after touchdown was scored by Ray "Scooter" MacLean, a Chicago Bears back.

1943

The last scoreless tie in the NFL was played between the New York Giants and the Detroit Lions at Briggs Stadium in Detroit.

1945

In his last season, Green Bay Packer end Don Hutson caught 47 passes, scored 10 touchdowns, and kicked 31 of 35 extra points.

1950

The last championship game for which any player received less than $1,000 was played. The winning Cleveland Browns received $1,113 and the losing Los Angeles Rams were paid $686.

1951

The last team to use the single wing formation was the Pittsburgh Steelers.

1952

The Dallas Texans became the last team to go out of business.

1962

Center Chuck Bednarik of the Philadelphia Eagles retired as the last NFL two-way player (both offense and defense).

1964

Jeff Richardson, the tackle of the Boston Patriots, was the last lineman to play without a face mask.

1966

Ollie Matson, a back with the Philadelphia Eagles, retired as the last player to make all-pro on both offense and defense.

1976

The last College All-Star Game was shortened by a thunderstorm.

The last winless team was the Tampa Bay Buccaneers.

1979

End Jim Marshall of the Minnesota Vikings ended his consecutive game playing streak at 302.

1983

The last NFL game was played in New York City. The Giants and the Jets both moved to New Jersey the next year.

7
The Teams

The National Football League today consists of twenty-eight teams — fourteen in the National Conference and fourteen in the American Conference. But it was not always so. The number of teams in the league has fluctuated greatly since its founding. The league started with twelve teams and, over the years, it has hit a high of twenty-eight teams and a low of eight. Here they are, grouped by states, with their teams and years.

Arizona
Phoenix
Cardinals — 1988-present

California
Los Angeles
Buccaneers — 1926
Rams — 1946-present
Raiders — 1982-present .

Oakland
Raiders — 1980-81

San Diego
Chargers — 1961-present

San Francisco
49ers — 1946-present

Colorado
Denver
Broncos — 1960-present

Connecticut
Hartford
Blues — 1926

District of Columbia
Washington
Redskins — 1937-present

Florida
Miami
Dolphins — 1966-present

Tampa
Tampa Bay Buccaneers — 1976-present

Georgia
Atlanta
Falcons — 1966-present

Illinois
Chicago
Cardinals — 1920-59
Tigers — 1920
Staleys — 1921
Bears — 1922-present

Decatur
Staleys — 1920

Rock Island
Independents — 1920-26

Indiana
Evansville
Crimson Giants — 1921-22

Hammond
Pros — 1920-26

Indianapolis
Colts — 1984-present

Muncie
Flyers — 1920-21

Kentucky
Louisville
Brecks — 1921-23
Colonels — 1926

Louisiana
New Orleans
Saints — 1967-present

Maryland
Baltimore
Colts — 1947-50
Colts — 1953-83

Massachusetts
Boston
Bulldogs — 1929
Braves — 1932
Redskins — 1933-36
Yanks — 1944-48
Patriots — 1960-70

Foxboro
New England Patriots —
    1971-present

Michigan
Detroit
Heralds — 1920-21
Panthers — 1925-26
Wolverines — 1928
Lions — 1934-present

Minnesota
Duluth
Kelleys — 1923-25
Eskimos — 1926-27

Minneapolis
Marines — 1922-24
Redjackets — 1929-30
Minnesota Vikings — 1961
    present

Missouri
Kansas City
Blues — 1924
Cowboys — 1925-26
Chiefs — 1963-present

St. Louis
All-Stars — 1923
Gunners — 1934
Cardinals — 1960-87

New Jersey
Newark
Tornadoes — 1930

Orange
Tornadoes — 1929

New York
Brooklyn
Lions — 1926
Dodgers — 1930-43
Tigers — 1944

Buffalo
All-Americans — 1921-23
Bisons — 1924-25
Rangers — 1926
Bisons — 1927
Bisons — 1929
Bills — 1960-present

New York City
Brinckley's Giants — 1921
Giants — 1925-present
Yankees — 1926-28
Bulldogs — 1949
Yanks — 1950-51
Jets — 1963-present

Rochester
Jeffersons — 1920-25

Stapleton
Staten Island Stapletons —
    1929-32

Tonawanda
Kardex — 1921

Ohio
Akron
Pros — 1920-25
Indians — 1926

Canton
Bulldogs — 1920-23
Bulldogs — 1925-26

Cincinnati
Celts — 1921
Reds — 1933-34
Bengals — 1968-present

Cleveland
Tigers — 1920-21
Indians — 1923
Bulldogs — 1924-25
Bulldogs — 1927
Indians — 1931

Rams — 1936-42
Rams — 1944-45
Browns — 1946-present

Columbus
Panhandles — 1920-22
Tigers — 1923-26

Dayton
Triangles — 1920-29

Marion
Oorang Indians — 1922-23

Portsmouth
Spartans — 1930-33

Toledo
Maroons — 1922-23

Pennsylvania
Frankford
Yellow Jackets — 1924-31

Philadelphia
Eagles — 1933-present

Pittsburgh
Pirates — 1933-39
Steelers — 1940-present

Pottsville
Maroons — 1925-28

Rhode Island
Providence
Steam Roller — 1925-31

Texas
Dallas
Texans — 1952
Texans — 1960-62
Cowboys — 1960-present

Houston
Oilers — 1960-present

Washington
Seattle
Seahawks — 1976-present

Wisconsin
Green Bay
Packers — 1921-present

Kenosha
Maroons — 1924

Milwaukee
Badgers — 1922-26
Racine
Legion — 1922-24
Tornadoes — 1926

But now the number of teams seems relatively stable. Here are some facts on the present day NFL teams. First of all, the address of the league office is 410 Park Avenue, New York, NY 10022.

National Conference

Eastern Division

Cardinals
P.O. Box 888
Phoenix, AZ 85001

The Cardinals play their home games in Tempe, Arizona, at Sun Devil Stadium, which seats 72,608. The Cardinals franchise is the oldest continuing team in the NFL. They began as the Racine Cardinals (named after a Chicago street, not a Wisconsin town). From 1920 to 1921, they played at Normal Field, moving to Comiskey Park from 1922-25, back to Normal Field from 1926 to 1928, and back to Comiskey Park from 1929 to 1959. In

1960, they moved to St. Louis, playing in Busch Stadium from 1960 to 1965, and then to Busch Memorial Stadium from 1966 to 1987. In 1988, they moved to Arizona.

Cowboys

One Cowboys Parkway
Irving, TX 75063

The Cowboys play their home games in Irving, Texas, at Texas Stadium, which seats 65,024.

In 1960, the team got an NFL franchise and played their games in the Cotton Bowl in Dallas. In 1970, they moved to the new Texas Stadium.

Eagles

Veterans Stadium
Broad Street and Pattison Avenue
Philadelphia, PA 19148

The Eagles play their home games in Philadelphia at Veterans Stadium, which seats 65,356.

The Eagles joined the NFL in 1933. Before that they had been the Frankford (Pennsylvania) Yellow Jackets. They were a team that kept changing home fields. First they were in Baker Bowl from 1933 to 1935. Then it was Municipal Stadium (1936-39), Shibe Park (1940), Municipal Stadium again (1941), Shibe Park (1942), and Pittsburgh's Forbes Park in 1943, when they merged with the Steelers as the Steagles for one year. Then it was back to Shibe Park (1944-57), Franklin Field of the University of Pennsylvania (1958-70), and finally Veterans Stadium in 1971.

Giants

Giants Stadium
East Rutherford, NJ 07073

The Giants play their home games in East Rutherford, New Jersey, in Giants Stadium, which seats 77,311.

The Giants joined the NFL in 1925, playing at the Polo Grounds until 1955. They switched to Yankee Stadium (1956-73), then to the Yale Bowl in New Haven, Connecticut (1973-74). After a one-year stay at Shea Stadium (1976), they moved to East Rutherford, New Jersey, upon the completion of Giants Stadium.

Redskins

Redskin Park Drive
Ashburn, VA 22011

The Redskins play their home games in RFK Stadium, which seats 55,683.

The Redskins began in 1932 as the Boston Braves, playing at Braves Field. In 1933, after changing their name to the Boston Redskins, they moved to Fenway Park, where they stayed until 1936. In 1937, they moved to the nation's capital, becoming the Washington Redskins and playing in

Griffith Stadium until the end of the 1960 season. In 1961, they moved into D.C. Stadium. In 1972, the name of the stadium was changed to RFK Stadium in honor of the assassinated Robert F. Kennedy.

Central Division
Bears
250 North Washington Road
Lake Forest, IL 60045

The Bears play their home games in Chicago at Soldier Field, which seats 66,946.

The Bears began as the Decatur (Illinois) Staleys in 1920. In 1921, the team was given to Coach George Halas and his partner, Dutch Sternaman. They moved the team to Chicago, where they played at Wrigley Field until 1970. In 1922, the Chicago Staleys became the Chicago Bears, and along the way they earned the nickname of "The Monsters of the Midway."

Buccaneers
One Buccaneer Place
Tampa, FL 33607

The Buccaneers play their home games in Tampa Stadium, which seats 74,315.

The team joined the NFL as an expansion club in 1976.

Lions
1200 Featherstone Road
Box 4200
Pontiac, MI 48342

The Lions play their home games in the Pontiac Silverdome in Pontiac, Michigan, which seats 80,500.

The team began as the Portsmouth (Ohio) Spartans in 1930, where they played in Spartan Stadium. In 1934, the Spartans moved to Detroit, becoming the Detroit Lions, where they played in the University of Detroit Stadium until 1937. From 1938 until 1974 they were located in Briggs Stadium (later renamed Tiger Stadium). When the Silverdome was completed in 1975, the Lions moved in.

Packers
1265 Lombardi Avenue
Green Bay, WI 54307

The Packers play home games at Lambeau Field in Green Bay, which seats 59,543. A few games are played at Milwaukee's County Stadium, which seats 56,051.

The team joined the NFL in 1921 and played in Hagemeister Brewery Park through the end of the 1922 season. They moved to Bellevue Park from 1923 to 1924, and then to the new City Stadium (which seated only 6,000) from 1925 to 1956. In 1933, the team was bought by local citizens, and it still belongs to townspeople. In 1957, Lambeau Field was inaugurated.

Vikings
9520 Viking Drive
Eden Prairie, MN 55344

The team plays its home games in the Hubert H. Humphrey Metrodome in Minneapolis, which seats 63,000.

The Vikings joined the NFL as an expansion team in 1961, playing in the Metropolitan Stadium in Bloomington, Minnesota, until 1981. In 1982, the Metrodome was completed and the Vikings moved in.

Western Division

Falcons
I-85 and Suwanee Road
Suwanee, GA 30175

The Falcons play their home games in the Georgia Dome, which seats 71,500.

The team joined the NFL in 1966 as an expansion club.

49ers
4949 Centennial Boulevard
Santa Clara, CA 95054

The team plays its home games in Candlestick Park in San Francisco, which seats 66,455.

The 49ers entered the league in 1950, coming from the old All-American Football Conference. From 1946 to 1970, they played in Kezar Stadium.

Rams
2327 West Lincoln Avenue
Anaheim, CA 92801

The team plays home games in Anaheim Stadium in Anaheim, California, which seats 69,008.

The Rams began in Ohio as the Cleveland Rams in 1937. They played in Municipal Stadium from 1937 to 1945, except for a year of suspended operations. Even though they won the league championship in 1945, they moved to Los Angeles because they were losing money in Cleveland. From 1946 to 1979, they played in the Los Angeles Memorial Coliseum, moving to Anaheim in 1980.

Saints
1500 Poydras Street
New Orleans, LA 70112

The team plays home games in the Louisiana Superdome, which seats 69,065.

The Saints joined the league in 1967 as an expansion team, and played in Tulane Stadium until 1974. They moved to the Superdome in 1975.

AMERICAN CONFERENCE

Eastern Division

Bills

One Bills Drive
Orchard Park, NY 14127

The team plays home games in Orchard Park, New York, in Rich Stadium, which seats 80,290.

The Bills have been members of the American Football League since 1960, when they began playing in War Memorial Stadium. With the official merger in 1970, they became members of the NFL. They moved to Rich Stadium in 1973.

Colts

P.O. Box 535000
Indianapolis, IN 45253

The team plays its home games in the Hoosier Dome, which seats 60,129.

The Colts began in Baltimore in the old All-American Conference in 1946. With the 1950 merger, the team joined the NFL. From 1953 to 1983, they played in Baltimore's Memorial Stadium. In 1984, the team was moved to Indianapolis and the Hoosier Dome.

Dolphins

Joe Robbie Stadium
2269 N.W. 199 Street
Miami, FL 33056

The team plays its home games in Joe Robbie Stadium, which seats 73,000.

The Dolphins entered the American Football League in 1966. With the 1970 merger, they became a part of the NFL. From 1966 to 1986, they played in Miami's Orange Bowl, then moved to the new Joe Robbie Stadium in 1987.

Jets

1000 Fulton Avenue
Hempstead, NY 11550

The team plays its home games in East Rutherford, New Jersey, in Giants Stadium, which seats 76,891.

The Jets were the New York Titans of the American Football League from 1960 to 1963, when the franchise was purchased and renamed the New York Jets. From 1960 to 1963, the team played at the Polo Grounds. They moved to Shea Stadium in 1964, finally settling in Giants Stadium in 1984.

Patriots

Foxboro Stadium

Route 1

Foxboro, MA 02035

The team plays its home games in Foxboro Stadium, which seats 60,794.

The Patriots began as the Boston Patriots of the American Football League in 1960. They played in Nickerson Field of Boston University (1960-62), Fenway Park (1963-68), Alumni Stadium of Boston College (1969), and Harvard Stadium (1970). In 1971, they moved to Foxboro Stadium, and renamed themselves the New England Patriots.

Central Division

Bengals

200 Riverfront Stadium

Cincinnati, OH 45202

The team plays its home games in Riverfront Stadium, which seats 60,389.

The Bengals entered the American Football League in 1968, and with the merger, they became an NFL club in 1970. From 1968 to 1969, they played in Nippert Stadium of the University of Cincinnati. The Bengals moved to Riverfront Stadium in 1970.

Browns

Cleveland Stadium

Cleveland, OH 44114

The team plays its home games in Cleveland Stadium, which seats 80,098.

The Browns began playing in the All-America Conference in 1946, and with the merger in 1950, they became members of the NFL.

Oilers

6910 Fannin

Houston, TX 77030

The team plays in the Astrodome, which seats 60,502.

The Oilers joined the American Football League in 1960, and, after the merger of 1970, they were official members of the NFL. From 1960 to 1964, they played in Jeppesen Stadium. The Oilers relocated to Rice Stadium of Rice University from 1965 to 1967. Then they moved into the Astrodome in 1968.

Steelers

Three Rivers Stadium

300 Stadium Circle

Pittsburgh, PA 15212

The team plays its home games in Three Rivers Stadium, which seats 59,492.

In 1933, Art Rooney got an NFL franchise for Pittsburgh, and he named his team the Pirates. Legend has it that he used the money he had won at the race track to finance the purchase, but that is suspicious. The Pirates played at Forbes Field in Pittsburgh from 1933 to 1957. In 1941, they were renamed the Steelers. From 1958 to 1963, they divided their time between Forbes Field and Pitt Stadium of the University of Pittsburgh. Then it was exclusively Pitt Stadium (1964-69), and finally, in 1970, they moved into the new Three Rivers Stadium.

Western Division
Broncos
13665 Broncos Parkway
Englewood, CO 80112
The team plays its home games in Mile High Stadium, which seats 76,273

The Broncos joined the American Football League as a charter member in 1960, moving into Mile High Stadium. In the 1970 merger, they became members of the NFL.

Chargers
San Diego Jack Murphy Stadium
P.O. Box 609609
San Diego, CA 92160
The team plays its home games in San Diego Jack Murphy Stadium, which seats 60,835.

The Chargers were charter members of the American Football League in 1960, but at the time they were the Los Angeles Chargers and played in Los Angeles Memorial Stadium. They moved to San Diego in 1961, playing in Balboa Stadium from 1961 to 1966. In 1967, they moved into the new San Diego Jack Murphy Stadium.

Chiefs
One Arrowhead Drive
Kansas City, MO 64129
The team plays its home games in Arrowhead Stadium, which seats 78,067.

The Chiefs began as the Dallas Texans, a team that lasted only a half-season in 1960 before selling its franchise back to the league. From 1960 to 1962, the Texans played their American Football League games in the Cotton Bowl in Dallas. In 1963, the Texans moved to Kansas City and became the Chiefs, playing in Municipal Stadium until 1971. The Chiefs became members of the NFL in the merger of 1970 and moved to Arrowhead Stadium in 1972.

Raiders
332 Center Street
El Segundo, CA 90245

The team plays its home games in the Los Angeles Memorial Coliseum, which seats 92,488.

The Raiders began as the Oakland Raiders when they were charter members of the American Football League. They played their home games in Kezar Stadium in San Francisco in 1960, but moved to San Francisco's Candlestick Park for the 1961 season. From 1962 to 1965, they played at Frank Youell Field in Oakland, and then, from 1966 to 1981, in the Oakland-Alameda County Coliseum. In the 1970 merger, they became full members of the NFL. In 1982, they moved to Los Angeles and began playing in the Los Angeles Memorial Coliseum.

Seahawks
11220 N.E. 53rd Street
Kirkland, WA 98033

The team plays its home games in The Kingdome, which seats 64,984.

The Seahawks began in 1976 as an expansion team playing in The Kingdome.

TRAINING CAMPS

All NFL teams have training camps that are used in the summer. Here are their locations.

Bears — University of Wisconsin-Platteville

Bengals — Wilmington College, Wilmington, Ohio

Bills — Fredonia, New York

Broncos — Northern Colorado University, Greeley

Browns — Lakeland Community College, Mentor, Ohio

Buccaneers — University of Tampa

Cardinals — Northern Arizona University, Flagstaff

Chargers — University of California-San Diego at La Jolla

Chiefs — University of Wisconsin-River Falls

Colts — Anderson University, Anderson, Indiana

Cowboys — St. Edward's University, Austin, Texas

Dolphins — St. Thomas University, Miami, Florida

Eagles — West Chester University, West Chester, Pennsylvania

Falcons — Suwanee, Georgia

49ers — Sierra Community College, Rocklin, California

Giants — Fairleigh Dickinson University, Madison, New Jersey

Jets — Hofstra University, Hempstead, New York

Lions — Pontiac Silverdome, Pontiac, Michigan

Oilers — Trinity University, San Antonio, Texas

Packers — St. Norbert College, West DePere, Wisconsin

Patriots — Bryant College, Smithfield, Rhode Island

Raiders — Radisson Hotel, Oxnard, California
Rams — University of California, Irvine
Redskins — Dickinson College, Carlisle, Pennsylvania
Saints — University of Wisconsin-La Crosse
Seahawks — Kirkland, Washington
Steelers — St. Vincent College, Latrobe, Pennsylvania
Vikings — Mankato State University, Mankato, Minnesota

COLORS

All NFL teams have official colors. Here they are:
Bears — navy blue, orange, and white
Bengals — black, orange, and white
Bills — royal blue, scarlet red, and white
Broncos — orange, blue, and white
Browns — seal brown, orange, and white
Buccaneers — Florida orange, white, and red
Cardinals — cardinal red, black, and white
Chargers — blue, gold, and white
Chiefs — red, gold, and white
Colts — royal blue, white, and silver
Cowboys — royal blue, metallic blue, silver, and white
Dolphins — aqua, coral, and white
Eagles — Kelly green, silver, and white
Falcons — red, black, and silver
49ers — Forty-Niners gold and scarlet
Giants — blue, red, and white
Jets — Kelly green and white
Lions — Honolulu blue and silver
Oilers — Columbia blue, scarlet, and white
Packers — dark green, gold, and white
Patriots — red, white, and blue
Raiders — silver and black
Rams — royal blue, gold, and white
Redskins — burgundy and gold
Saints — old gold, black, and white
Seahawks — blue, green, and silver
Steelers — black and gold
Vikings — purple, gold, and white

FIRST COACHES

Here are the men who led the teams in their first year.

Bears — George Halas

Bengals — Paul Brown

Bills — Garrard "Buster" Ramsey

Broncos — Frank Filchock

Browns — Paul Brown

Buccaneers — John McKay

Cardinals — Paddy Driscoll

Chargers — Sid Gilman

Chiefs — Hank Stram

Colts — Cecil Isbell

Cowboys — Tom Landry

Dolphins — George Wilson

Eagles — Lud Wray

Falcons — Norb Hecker

49ers — Buck Shaw

Giants — Bob Folwell

Jets — Sammy Baugh

Lions — Potsy Clark

Oilers — Lou Rymkus

Packers — Curly Lambeau

Patriots — Lou Saban

Raiders — Eddie Erdelatz

Rams — Hugo Bezdek

Redskins — Lud Wray

Saints — Tom Fears

Seahawks — Jack Patera

Steelers — Forrest Douds

Vikings — Norm Van Brocklin

8
What Did They Say?

Football people throughout history have always had something to say. They have felt called upon to offer their reading or listening public some pithy comments. Here are a few gems.

NAY-SAYERS

In the beginning of professional football, some prominent sportsmen had some awful things to say about playing for pay.

Earl "Red" Blake
College football coach most notable for his tenure at the United States Military Academy

When asked if he had enjoyed the game he had just seen — a 1950 game between the Yankees and the Browns: "Yes, but it wasn't football. Football is a college game. It calls for three things: youth, condition, spirit, plus continuous hard work by coaches as well as players. Nothing is wrong with professional football. It's what it aims to be. It's a show. The pros are in the entertainment business ... I think a good pro team might get itself up to beat a good college team in a single game. But if the pro team were put into a league with good college teams — like Notre Dame, Michigan, Ohio State, Oklahoma, Southern California, Tennessee, and Texas — it would have to learn to play football the way the colleges do or it wouldn't stand a chance. A fiery team like Tennessee would cripple a pro club."

Major John L. Griffith
Former Commissioner of the Big Ten college football conference

"Professional baseball is killing the game in the colleges and universities, and professional football will have the same effect on the king of college sports. If professional football continues to grow, then the colleges must find some other sort of games which will fill the large stadiums."

Amos Alonzo Stagg
Pioneer college football coach, most notably of the University of Chicago

"And now comes along another serious menace, possibly greater than all others, *viz.* Sunday professional football ... to cooperate with Sunday professional football games is to cooperate with forces which are destructive of the finest elements of interscholastic and intercollegiate football and to add to the heavy burden of the schools and colleges in preserving it in its ennobling worth."

PROFESSIONAL COACHES

Jimmy Conzelman
Former coach of the Chicago Cardinals

On rival Bears coach, George Halas: "He is the nicest rich man I know."

After his Cardinals had lost badly to the Bears: "Don't get the idea that being beaten by the Bears 42-12 bothered me a bit. Oh, not in the least. I went home after the game, had a good night's rest and a very hearty breakfast. I said good-bye to the Missus, and strolled down the hall to the elevator, whistling a light tune. I pushed the elevator bell and took in my profile in the hall mirror. I was a picture of elegance in my Cavenaugh hat, tweed sports jacket, and well-shined tan shoes. Then I went back to my apartment and put on my trousers."

Mike Ditka
Chicago Bears coach

Asked why the Bears have done so well at the beginning of the season: "I guess it's because September ends with an 'r'."

After a 41-13 loss to the Minnesota Vikings: "Once the truck hit me, I did not bother getting up. I just lay there and watched."

Asked if he planned to be more laid back in the future: "Of course. Last week I slept through the entire third quarter."

Jerry Glanville
Atlanta Falcons coach

On the hazards of coaching: "If you're a pro coach, NFL stands for 'Not for Long.'"

After the Falcons lost to the Philadelphia Eagles, 24-23: "I stopped at a Burger King window on the way home with my wife and my son. The guy at the window had been at the game. He, too, had suffered. I could tell because he didn't fix it my way."

On the Falcons' locker room actions after they had beaten the San Francisco 49ers twice in 1991: "The 49ers call us the boom box because they can hear us over there [in the other locker room]. We play songs and dance before we come out. They're over there sitting, staring at their lockers. They said, 'How could the Boom Box beat us twice?' Well, isn't *that* special?"

On the NFL's rules barring touchdown celebrations by players: "They want to open the oven and have every cookie look the same. These are football players. They're human. They've got emotions. Let 'em dance."

Bud Grant
Former Minnesota Vikings coach

On coaching: "A good coach needs a patient wife, loyal dog, and a great quarterback — not necessarily in that order."

George Halas
Former owner-coach of the Chicago Bears

On his retirement: "I knew it was time to quit when I was chewing out an official and he walked off the penalty faster than I could keep up with him."

On professional football: "Professional football will never replace college football, and we don't want it to."

Lindy Infante
Former Green Bay Packers coach

After a 6-10 season in 1990: "I won't have to run around the country and collect a bunch of Coach of the Year trophies."

Curly Lambeau
Former Green Bay Packers coach

On his coaching: "I think better when I'm excited."

After he had fined a lineman $500 for missing practice and had had the lineman threaten to kill him if he cashed the check: "It won't do any good. It would merely cost you another $500."

Tom Landry
Former coach of the Dallas Cowboys

On football: "Football is an incredible game. Sometimes it's so incredible, it's unbelievable."

Vince Lombardi
Former coach of the Green Bay Packers and Washington Redskins

To his players: "If you aren't fired with enthusiasm, you will be fired with enthusiasm."

John Madden
Former coach of the Oakland Raiders

Asked if modern players are overpaid: "A lot of us are overpaid."

Dave McGinnis
Linebacker coach of the Chicago Bears

On stopping the Detroit Lions offense: "The key to Detroit's run-'n-shoot is when Barry Sanders runs, you shoot him."

Greasy Neale
Former Philadelphia Eagles coach

Asked if he had borrowed the T formation from the Chicago Bears: "No. I stole it."

Chuck Noll
Former coach of the Pittsburgh Steelers

On his future: "If I could see into the future, I'd be at the race track today."

On his coaching: "Just put me down as a teacher. Don't ever call me a winner. Players win, coaches teach. I was a teacher."

On scrambling quarterbacks: "We don't want jazz musicians. We want classical musicians."

Steve Owen
Former coach of the New York Giants

On coaching: "The best offense can be built around ten basic plays. Defense can be built on two. All the rest is razzle-dazzle, egomania, and box office."

After a 1952 63-7 loss to the Pittsburgh Steelers: "It's a good thing I'm known as a defensive genius, or the score would have been 100-7."

After coach Greasy Neale of the Philadelphia Eagles had collapsed on the opposite sidelines: "I always knew I would see one of us coaches go that way. I have felt like that myself. But Neale was all right — he was cursing me and my Giants as he crawled into the ambulance."

Bill Parcells
Former coach of the New York Giants

Asked, just before Super Bowl XXV, if he feared the opposing quarterback: "Let me tell you what I'm scared of: spiders, snakes and the IRS."

Asked about his reputation as a motivator: "If you win, you're a great motivator. If you lose, you don't know what you're doing."

Jimmy Phelan
Former coach of the 1952 Dallas Texans

When his team was trailing the Detroit Lions, 41-0, with a few minutes to go, and the Texans scored: "Okay, boys, we got 'em on the run now."

John Ralston
Former coach of the Denver Broncos

On leaving as coach: "I left because of illness and fatigue. The fans were sick and tired of me."

Hank Stram
Former coach of the Kansas City Chiefs

On coaching: "When I got into coaching, I knew I was getting into a high-risk profession. So I adopted the philosophy that yesterday is a cancelled check, today is cash on the line, and tomorrow is a promissory note."

Richard Williamson
Former Tampa Bay Buccaneers coach

Reporting on the magnetic resonance imaging test [a medical diagnostic test] given to a player: "He had the MRI two weeks ago. MRI — did I pronounce that right?"

PLAYERS

Mike Baab
Cleveland Browns center

On his team's defensive backfield: "Our defensive backs were like a river. There was a lot more activity at the mouth than at the source."

Sammy Baugh
Washington Redskins quarterback

On becoming a movie hero: "I can see it coming already. Some big guy is going to knock me down and then give me his hand and say, 'Mister Barrymore, can I assist you to your feet?'"

George Blanda
Oakland Raiders quarterback/kicker

On his coach: "Of all the coaches I've ever played for, John Madden was the kindest and most thoughtful."

Terry Bradshaw
Pittsburgh Steelers quarterback

On passing: "If a receiver's open, throw to him. If he's not, throw to him anyway. Let the guy show his athletic ability."

Eric Dickerson
Indianapolis Colts running back

On growing old: "If I've lost a step, it's a step a lot of other guys never had."

Mike Ditka
Chicago Bears end

On the stinginess of his coach, George Halas: "He throws nickels around like manhole covers."

Walt Garrison
Dallas Cowboys back

Asked if his coach, Tom Landry, ever smiled: "I don't know. I only played there nine years."

Pete Gent
Dallas Cowboys flanker

On being informed that he was being moved from one side of the line to the other in a Philadelphia Eagles game: "You mean ... I'm going to play for Philadelphia?"

Otto Graham
Cleveland Browns quarterback

On quarterbacking: "We just hand the ball off to somebody else and let them do the work and get the credit for it."

Ray Green
Cleveland Browns wide receiver

On becoming a veteran: "Maybe I have lost a step, but I had a few to lose."

Dan Hampton
Chicago Bears defensive lineman

On Giants Stadium: "A nuclear wasteland that they built a stadium on."

On his retirement after twelve years and nine knee operations and his last game was a 1990 defeat by the New York Giants in the play-offs, 31-3: "It was a fairy tale that ended in a train wreck."

Cal Hubbard
Green Bay Packers tackle

On his coach, Curly Lambeau: "If that buzzard ever died, they'd have trouble finding six guys to volunteer as pallbearers."

On intimidating his opponents: "You see those two holes over the ears in the helmet? Well, they're not to hear through. They're for you to stick your fingers in his helmet and jerk his face down when you raise your knee up."

Joe Jacoby
Washington Redskins lineman

On fans who attend games wearing pig snouts: "The really scary thing is that some of these people work for the government."

Deacon Jones
Los Angeles Rams end

On why he invented the term "sack": "It took up too much room in headlines to say that a player tackled the quarterback behind the line of scrimmage. I liked sack, because, like you know, you sack a city — you devastate it."

Henry Jordan
Green Bay Packers quarterback

Asked how Packers coach Vince Lombardi treated his players: "He treated us all alike — like dogs."

Alex Karras
Detroit Lions lineman

On becoming an actor: "I was getting paid $90,000 a year to play football, and I got $17,000 to shoot a commercial that took an hour and a half. That's when I figured it all out."

Bucko Kilroy
Philadelphia Eagles tackle

On Les Bingaman, the 350-pound Detroit Lions guard: "They had to take him to the general store to weigh him."

Pat Leahy
New York Jets place-kicker

On what part of the body is the first to go as an athlete gets older: "It's the hair."

Max McGee
Green Bay Packers end

On his coach, Vince Lombardi: "When he says 'sit down,' I don't even bother to look for a chair."

Don Meredith
Dallas Cowboys quarterback

On the ferociously cold, snowy, and windy game in Green Bay in 1967: "All I have to say is there was trouble on every corner and it just didn't seem like Christmas out there."

On his coach, Tom Landry: "Tom Landry is a perfectionist. If he was married to Raquel Welch, he'd expect her to cook."

Joe Namath
New York Jets quarterback

On his unique white shoes: "Actually they were sitting in my locker when I joined the Jets. I used to tape my shoes with white tape when I was at Alabama. I guess they figured I liked the color. We used to joke that [coach] Weeb Ewbank ordered those shoes to save money on the tape. But I liked them, so I wore them. You know, I still wear white shoes, almost all the time. I've run into Pat Boone a few times, and I figure if it's good enough for him, it's good enough for me."

Nate Newton
Dallas Cowboys tackle

After a 1991 24-0 loss to the Philadelphia Eagles, who sacked Dallas quarterback Troy Aikman eleven times: "They were hitting us from everywhere. I felt like I was at Pearl Harbor."

John Riggins
Washington Redskins running back

After gaining 166 yards rushing in Super Bowl XVII: "Reagan may be president, but I'm the king."

After sitting out the 1980 season: "I'm bored, I'm broke, and I'm back."

Emmitt Smith
Dallas Cowboys back

After rushing thirty-two times for 112 yards and catching six passes for thirty-six yards in a victory over the Cleveland Browns: "Thirty-two carries? I'm only twenty-two. I want to live to see twenty-three."

Lawrence Taylor
New York Giants linebacker

On his coach, Bill Parcells: "He thinks he's the master psychologist. He always has little sly comments that if he wasn't the head coach, you'd want to punch him. But we play hard for each other. The last thing you want to see is Bill moping like somebody took his bag of M&M's."

Joe Theismann
Washington Redskins quarterback

On football brains: "The word *genius* isn't applicable in football. A genius is a guy like Norman Einstein."

Duane Thomas
Dallas Cowboys running back

On the Super Bowl: "If the Super Bowl is the ultimate game, why do they play it every year?"

After gaining ninety-five yards and scoring a touchdown to beat the Miami Dolphins and being asked if he were as fast as he had looked during the game: "Evidently."

Jim Thorpe
New York Giants back

After being called the greatest athlete in the world by King Gustav V of Sweden: "Thanks, King."

Bulldog Turner
Chicago Bears center

On how to best the weekly weigh-in: "Always wear a T-shirt and underwear. Just before getting on the scale, take off the T-shirt and nonchalantly place it at the left end of the balance arm. This will act as a counterweight and buy you several pounds. If that isn't enough, use the underwear, too. Be sure a friend follows you in line. When you step on the scale, have him put a finger under each of your buttocks and lift ever so gently. Be sure he's a good friend. Place your feet on the scale so that your big toes extend over the edge. Curl them over and push up."

Doak Walker
Detroit Lions back

On his quarterback, Bobby Layne: "He never lost a football game in his life, although once in a while time ran out on him."

Marvin Washington
New York Jets defensive end

After a win over the Cleveland Browns: "They knew that Elvis had left the building."

After a win over the Indianapolis Colts: "Why give them any blue sky on an otherwise cloudy day?"

On his future: "There are only two kinds of football players, those who have been cut and those who are going to be cut. Right now I happen to be among the latter."

Alvin Wright
Los Angeles Rams defensive tackle

After Rams defensive line coach, John Teerlinck, remembering a *Rocky* movie in which the hero chased a chicken to train for his fight with Apollo Creed, brought a chicken to practice for the defenders to chase it, and the chicken didn't move: "It's a laid-back California chicken."

EXECUTIVES

Anonymous
Tampa Bay Buccaneers official

After the new football club played its first game in Green Bay and he saw that the scoreboard listed his team as Tampa: "When they play us at home, we ought to put their name on our scoreboard as 'Green.'"

Lamar Hunt
President of the Kansas City Chiefs

On the naming of the Super Bowl: "Shannon, my seven-year-old daughter, had a toy called a super ball. In the AFL-NFL meetings, we had just referred to the 'final game.' ... One day I just happened to come out and call the game the 'Super Bowl.'"

Wellington Mara
New York Giants owner

On coaching: "Few die on the job."

Tex Schramm
Dallas Cowboys general manager

When the team unveiled their new 1954 uniforms: "[The color] is sort of blue-hued silver, sort of."

Sonny Werblin
New York Jets owner

On paying $427,000 for Joe Namath, a rookie: "A million dollar set is worthless if you put a $2,000 actor in the main role."

Edward Bennett Williams
Washington Redskins owner

On the spending habits of Coach George Allen: "I gave George an unlimited budget and he exceeded it."

George Young
New York Giants general manager

When the Super Bowl champions of 1990 fell to 2-3 in 1991: "The New York media and fans are becoming like Paris during the French Revolution. They need to see somebody go to the guillotine every day."

WRITERS

Anonymous
Minnesota sportswriter

On Vikings coach Bud Grant's icy demeanor: "I don't know whether to interview him or ski him."

Anonymous
Canton Morning Star *reporter*
On the football rivalry between the Canton Bulldogs and Massillon Tigers: "Money is no object and the players are getting big lumps for playing."

Pete Axthelm
Sports editor of Newsweek
On the celebrating Steelers after a Super Bowl victory: "I can't stand to look at a team that hasn't beaten the spread and thinks it's *won*."

Erma Bombeck
Syndicated columnist
On Thanksgiving Day football: "Thanksgiving dinners take eighteen hours to prepare, and they are consumed in twelve minutes. Halftime takes twelve minutes. This is no coincidence."

Don Daly and Bob O'Donnell
Sportswriters
Reasons why football is better than baseball:
1. You can just *watch* football. You don't have to 'celebrate it.'
2. Norm Cash won the 1961 American League batting title with a bat that had a cork in it. Gale Sayers won the 1969 NFL rushing title with a knee that had no cartilage in it.
3. Fall afternoons are better than summer afternoons.
4. You can't intentionally walk Joe Montana.
5. When a baseball player hits a home run he jogs around the bases. When a football player scores a touchdown he runs for his life.
6. The defense can score in football.
7. Bad football teams play 16 games. Bad baseball teams play 162.
8. There are no 1-0 games.
9. Passing a football is much more difficult than pitching a baseball.
10. Our Pop Warner teams can beat Taiwan's any day.
11. There's no balk rule to explain.
12. NFL commissioners have names like Bert, Pete, and Paul. Baseball's go by the names of Bowie, Bartlett, and Fay.
13. Burt Lancaster played Jim Thorpe. William Bendix played Babe Ruth.
14. There were four blacks in professional football before there was one in major league baseball.
15. Football players don't play golf the morning of a night game.
16. Football coaches don't wear uniforms.
17. Football players are, almost without exception, college-educated.
18. In football, as in life, the ball doesn't always bounce predictably.

Pete Gent
Reporter and novelist

To a Dallas Cowboys rookie who was reading coach Tom Landry's play book: "Don't bother reading it, kid. Everybody gets killed in the end."

Don Pierson
Chicago Tribune *sportswriter*

On Coach Paul Brown: "Brown turned coaching into a science. He was the first to use notebooks and classroom techniques extensively. He was the first to organize film study and player grades, intelligence tests, and an elaborate college scouting system. Brown invented the face mask. He was the first to send in plays with messenger guards. He tried to put radios into the helmets of his quarterbacks ... Brown was one of the first to split a halfback as a flanker to force the defense to spread. The draw play was his idea to slow the pass rush."

George Will
Political observer in magazines, in newspapers, and on television

On football: "Football combines two of the worst things about American life. It is violence punctuated by committee meetings.

MISCELLANEOUS PEOPLE

Anonymous
NFL referee

As he marched off a ten-yard penalty against the Chicago Bears for coach George Halas' coaching from the sidelines (then illegal), after Halas pointed out that the prescribed penalty was fifteen yards: "The kind of coaching you've been doing isn't worth fifteen yards."

Etty Allen
Wife of Washington Redskins coach George Allen

On her husband's diet: "I think the reason George likes ice cream is because he doesn't have to chew it. Chewing would take away his concentration from football."

Ralph Campbell
Member of the Hogettes male Washington Redskins cheerleaders

On the group's costumes: "Our designer is Calvin Swine."

Prince Charles
The Prince of Wales

Asked if he would be going to the World Bowl '91 game of the World League of American Football between the London Monarchs and the Barcelona Dragons: "What game?"

Mike Ditka
Chicago Bears coach and marketer of a cologne for men

On Mike Ditka Cologne: "You can be tough in the ways you have to be tough, but not in the way you smell."

Frank Gifford
Hall of Fame player and television football analyst

Remark during a Green Bay Packers game featuring icy temperatures, wind, and snow: "I think I'll have another bite of my coffee."

Harold "Red" Grange
Hall of Fame player and radio and television football analyst

On New York Giants tackle Tex Irvin: "He was so slow you could have timed him with a calendar."

Alex Karras
Detroit Lions defensive lineman, actor, television football analyst

Describing an Oakland Raider who had shaved his head: "That's Otis Sistrunk from the University of Mars."

On television commercials: "Once when I was still playing, there was a time-out. I said, 'Who called that?' You see, I was the captain, and I didn't call it. And they said, 'It was a commercial time-out. Goodyear Tires called it.' I loved it. It was beautiful. It's what America's all about."

On his broadcasting style: "I tried to be freewheeling. Once I said that a guy was so good he had gotten a Cadillac in college, and the control room went crazy. They screamed at me to remember that Ford was the game's sponsor and paid our salaries."

John Madden
Oakland Raiders coach and television football analyst

On his fear of flying: "I thought it was an inner ear infection that was aggravated by altitude, but then I realized that the anxiety would start as soon as the stewardess closed the door. One day I had a flight from Tampa to California with a stop in Houston. I got off there, checked into a hotel, and never flew again."

On today's players: "There are guys playing today that I don't think enjoy playing. They play for the money."

On the fans: "You can't really say who are the best fans. The Chicago fans are always *there*, win or lose, so you like that. And the New York fans are knowledgeable, and you like that. But I go for the complete scene in football. The best scene is Washington, RFK Stadium, the Redskins. You get in there, and it's real grass, and they're playing that great fight song, 'Hail to the Redskins,' and the whole place kind of rocks."

On his dislikes: "The three most phoney things in football are artificial turf, domed stadiums, and The Wave."

On staying in shape for television's football viewing season: "Lie around a lot. A mistake some people made in the summer was that they moved around too much. Just practice sitting for six, seven, hey ten or twelve hours. Do nothing. Then when you get the sitting point down, it's easy to put the game there in front of you."

On the importance of pacing yourself while watching television games: "Take it one game at a time, just like the coaches tell their players. Don't try to watch a bunch of games, don't look ahead to the big game, just get through the one you're watching."

On avoiding Sunday afternoon outings: "You say, 'just let me watch the first half.' Then you say, 'Well, it's a good game, we'll go right after it's over.' Before you know it, it's dark and the zoo is closed. Procrastinating by halves is better."

On how to reconnect with loved ones at the end of the season: "In February, start your recovery. Don't worry about relationships. Just get the blood flowing. Swing your arms. Stretch. In March or April, you can take care of birthdays, Mother's Day, and all that stuff. But remember: In July the NFL starts training camp. Then you have to start getting in shape to sit around for six or seven hours at a time again. Doubleheaders [in baseball] are a good place to start."

Bob Martin
Broadcaster

On Broncos general manager Dean Griffin's tight-fistedness: "[He was] the kind of guy who took off his glasses when he wasn't looking at anything."

Babe Ruth
Baseball hero

Advice to Harold "Red" Grange during Grange's first season as a professional football player: "Kid, don't believe anything they write about you, and don't pick up too many dinner checks."

Dorothy Shula
Wife of Miami Dolphins coach Don Shula

On her husband: "I'm fairly confident that if I died tomorrow, Don would find a way to preserve me until the season was over and he had time for a nice funeral."

Hank Stram
Kansas City Chiefs coach and television football commentator

On New Orleans Saints running back Craig Heyward: "He's like a runaway Winnebago: you can hit him, but you can't put your arms around him."

Sasha Kornilov
A fifteen-year-old Russian girl

On her impression of American football after watching it for the first time: "I think the form of the ball is interesting, and I like the way the players cling to each other."

9
Just Plain Trivia

In the more than seventy years since the beginning of professional football leagues, there have been a number of unusual events. Here are some little-known facts, plus some nostalgia.

LOSERS

After a game that ended in a 0-0 tie between the Decatur (Illinois) Staleys and the Rock Island (Illinois) Independents at Douglas Park in Rock Island, a mob chased the Staleys to their bus because they thought the team had played a dirty game.

The only NFL team to lose only one game in its history was the Tonawanda (New York) Kardex. They played only one game — in 1921 — and lost to the Rochester (New York) Jeffersons, 45-0.

The Oorang Indians were formed in LaRue, Ohio, and played their games in Marion, Ohio. They won only three games in their two years in the league (1922-23). To get fans in the stands, they scheduled entertainment before their games and at halftime. There were shooting exhibitions with dogs retrieving the targets; Indian dances; tomahawk and knife-throwing contests; and one player even wrestled a bear.

On October 17, 1923, all ten NFL games were shutouts, and three ended in 0-0 ties.

The 1925 Chicago Cardinals had the best record in the NFL at 11-2-1, better than the 10-2 Pottsville (Pennsylvania) Maroons. But the last two wins were over disbanded teams and owner Chris O'Brien refused the championship.

In 1926, there were 86 shutouts in the 116 NFL games, and ten of them were 0-0 ties.

The Cincinnati Bengals of the American Football League of the early 1940s had to forfeit a game because they were unable to come up with enough players.

The 1944 Card-Pitts (a combination of the Chicago Cardinals and the Pittsburgh Steelers) were nicknamed the "Carpets" because they lost all ten of their games.

On October 24, 1965, the Green Bay Packers beat the Dallas Cowboys 13-3, but both teams had negative passing records. Packers quarterback Bart Starr had -10 yards and Cowboys quarterback Craig Morton had -1. The reason was that Starr was sacked five times for -52 yards and Morton ten times for -62 yards.

The worst fifty-eight minutes occurred in an NFL game on October 27, 1991. Chicago Bears quarterback Jim Harbaugh completed only two of nineteen passes for sixteen yards. He also had had eleven consecutive interceptions. But in the last two minutes, he completed three of three passes for forty-five yards with no time-outs remaining, including a twelve-yarder for a touchdown, beating the New Orleans Saints, 20-17.

When the Atlanta Falcons beat the San Diego Chargers in San Diego in 1991, it ended a nineteen-road-game losing streak, which had lasted 1,029 days, was accomplished in thirteen states, and was witnessed by 1,044,323 fans.

Nine teams have never been in the Super Bowl — the Falcons, Browns, Lions, Oilers, Saints, Cardinals, Seahawks, Chargers, and Buccaneers.

The Minnesota Vikings and the Denver Broncos have each played in four Super Bowls and lost them all. But the Vikings record is the worst. In their four games, they have never had a lead, never scored in the first half, and never kicked a successful field goal.

The official score of a forfeited game is 1-0.

In 1921, eight members of the Buffalo All-Americans also played on Saturdays for the Philadelphia Quakers (a non-NFL team). Among them were back John Scott, end Heinie Miller, center Lud Wray, guard Joe Spagna, and tackle Lou Little.

PLAYERS

Steve Belichick, the Detroit Lions clubhouse boy, was put in as a punt receiver for one game in 1941. He handled only one punt, but ran it back seventy-seven yards for a touchdown.

Raymond Berry of the Baltimore Colts, one of the greatest ends in pro football, caught more passes for more yardage than any other player, but he was constantly teased about his average size, poor eyesight, and lack of speed.

Place-kicker Dean Biasucci of the Baltimore Colts once toured in a theatrical company, playing Mark Antony in *Julius Caesar*.

Terry Bradshaw, the Pittsburgh Steelers quarterback, went to the Steelers in 1970 after a coin toss with the Chicago Bears, who also wanted him.

Jim Castiglia, the Philadelphia Eagles blocking back, was hired by the Philadelphia Athletics baseball team as a batting practice and bullpen catcher.

Jack Christiansen, the Detroit Lions back, was the first to score two touchdowns on punt returns in a single game — he did it twice in 1951. The only others to do it were Dick Christy, the New York Titans back, in 1961, and Rick Upchurch, the Denver Broncos end, in 1976.

James Coley, the Chicago Bears tight end, and his wife, Gwannettia, have six children. The girls are named Ani, Fehlisegwanafay, Myrialysia, Shanuanevia, and Tiyonneteona. The one boy is named James.

George Halas, the owner of the Chicago Bears, once played end. He ran for ninety-eight yards with a recovered fumble, a record that stood for forty-nine years. But he was being chased by Jim Thorpe.

George Halas was only big enough to make the "lightweight team" at Crane High School in Chicago.

Chuck Howley, the Dallas Cowboys linebacker, was the only losing player to win the Super Bowl trophy as most valuable player. This was in Super Bowl V, where the Cowboys were beaten by the Baltimore Colts, 16-13. Howley recovered a fumble and caught two interceptions.

Cal Hubbard is the only man to be elected to both the Pro Football and Baseball Halls of Fame. He was a tackle with the New York Giants, Green Bay Packers, and Pittsburgh Pirates, as well as being a major league umpire.

Keith Jackson, the Philadelphia Eagles tight end, released a record album in 1991. It was a rap recording called "K-Jack-n-America," and the lyrics stressed social responsibility for young people. "Stay away from drugs, stay away from violence, and stay in school."

Ernie Ladd, the defensive tackle of the San Diego Chargers, Houston Oilers, and Kansas City Chiefs, ate 124 pancakes in a charity pancake-eating contest, using six containers of syrup to do the job. But he didn't win because he appeared late.

John Law, the tackle for the Newark (New Jersey) Tornadoes in 1930, appropriately enough, went on to coach the football team at Sing Sing Prison.

Gino Marchetti, the Baltimore Colts end, was the founder of Gino's Pizza.

George Musso, the Chicago Bears guard, played college football against two future presidents while he was at Millikin University — Gerald Ford (University of Michigan center) and Ronald Reagan (Eureka College guard).

The Nesser Brothers set a record as the most brothers ever to play for the same team at the same time. In 1920, Frank (back), Phil (guard), Fred (guard), John (back), and Ted (center) all played for the Columbus (Ohio) Panhandles.

Cal Rossi of the University of California was chosen by the Washington Redskins in 1946 as their first round draft pick. But the team hadn't done its homework. He was a junior and ineligible for the draft. The next year they chose him again, but their first round pick was again wasted, since he chose not to play professional football.

Frank Ryan, the quarterback of the Cleveland Browns, had a Ph.D. in mathematics and an IQ of 155. His doctoral dissertation was titled, "A Characterization of Asymptotic Values of a Function Holomorphic in the Unit Disc."

Don Shula, the coach of the Miami Dolphins, played for the Cleveland Browns, Baltimore Colts, and Washington Redskins as a back, and began his professional career in 1951 at a salary of $5,000 for the season.

Jan Stenerud played for the Kansas City Chiefs, Green Bay Packers, and Minnesota Vikings and was the first pure kicker to make the Hall of Fame (in 1991). He was born in Norway and came to the United States on a skiing scholarship from Montana State University.

Y.A. Tittle, the Hall of Fame quarterback of the Baltimore Colts, San Francisco 49ers, and New York Giants, played only two minutes in his first football game. It was in junior high school, and he was used as a fill-in while another player changed shoes.

Johnny Unitas, the Hall of Fame quarterback for the Baltimore Colts, graduated from the University of Louisville, but he was passed over in more than 200 draft choices in the NFL. He played sandlot football for a year and was chosen by the Pittsburgh Steelers in 1955. They cut him before he was able to play a single down, he went back home to play semi-pro football, and went to the Colts in 1956, signing for $7,000 his first year. Unitas holds the NFL record for most completed passes, but he also holds the record for most fumbles in a career.

COACHES

Hugo Bezdek was the only man to be an NFL coach and a baseball manager. He coached the Cleveland Rams (1937-38) and managed the Pittsburgh Pirates (1917-19).

Paul Brown is credited with the invention of the draw play. It was actually the result of a broken play by the Cleveland Browns in the late 1940s, when quarterback Otto Graham had to hand off to back Marion Motley. Brown caught it on the game films and instituted the play.

When Bears coach Mike Ditka introduced his new brand of cologne, it was available only in the Chicago area and cost $24 an ounce.

Buff Donelli was the only man to coach college and NFL football at the same time. In 1941, he was the coach of both the Pittsburgh Steelers and the Duquesne University teams.

Curly Lambeau, the coach of the Green Bay Packers, entered his team in the American Professional Football Association (later the NFL) with a payment of $50. But he used college players under assumed names and the Packers were kicked out of the league. Lambeau apologized and bought his way back into the league for $250, which he had borrowed.

Steelers coach Chuck Noll called George Atkinson of the Raiders a "dirty player" in 1976. He was fined $1,000 for the remark, but Atkinson was fined $1,500 for being a dirty player.

Chuck O'Brien organized the longest lasting franchise in the NFL in 1899. It was a neighborhood football team on the South Side of Chicago — the Morgan Athletic Club. The team later became the Normals and then the

Racine (after Racine Avenue) Cardinals, the Chicago Cardinals, the St. Louis Cardinals, and the Phoenix Cardinals.

Steve Owen was the coach of the New York Giants for more than twenty years (1931-53), yet he never had a formal contract.

Don Shula, the coach of the Miami Dolphins, received a suggestion from President Richard Nixon in 1973. Nixon suggested that a long down-and-out pass from quarterback Bob Griese to end Paul Warfield might help in the Super Bowl game. Shula tried it. It didn't work, and it may have cost the Dolphins the game.

Bob Snyder, the coach of the Los Angeles Rams, told his team at halftime of the final exhibition game: "If you don't do better in the second half, there are some people in this room who won't be on this club tomorrow night." He was right. That night he was fired.

Sam Wyche, coach of the Cincinnati Bengals, was in trouble during the 1991 season because they kept losing. Ever a fighter for the homeless, Wyche gave football fans a vote on his future, with canned goods ballots going to charities for the homeless. In supermarkets, shoppers were to drop canned goods in large containers labeled "Can the Coach" and "Don't Can the Coach." The food went to charity, but the coach left at the end of the season.

EXECUTIVES

Arthur Folz, manager of the Milwaukee Badgers in 1925, was the only man ever to be suspended for life from the NFL. He had used four high school players on the team. The franchise was also canceled that year.

Art McBride, owner of the Cleveland Browns in the 1940s, owned a taxicab company. Rather than risk losing the players he had to cut to meet the thirty-three-man roster, he gave them jobs driving cabs so that he could recall them in case of an injury to one of his regulars. That was the beginning of the term "Taxi Squad."

Art Rooney owned half of the Philadelphia Eagles in 1941. When Alexis Thompson bought half of the Pittsburgh Steelers, he traded with Rooney, and Rooney was able to return to Pittsburgh — the team he had once owned.

Danny Thomas, the television and night club comedian, was one of the first two owners of the Miami Dolphins.

NON-PLAYERS

Sixteen men who never played football in the NFL have been enshrined in the Pro Football Hall of Fame. Here they are:

Bert Bell — Commissioner, coach, owner

Charles Bidwell — Owner

Paul Brown — Coach, owner

Joe Carr — NFL president, founder, coach

Al Davis — Owner, coach
Weeb Ewbank — Coach
Sid Gilman — Coach
Lamar Hunt — AFL founder, owner
Vince Lombardi — Coach
George Preston Marshall — Owner

Tim Mara — Owner
Shorty Ray — League official
Dan Reeves — Owner
Art Rooney — Owner
Pete Rozelle — Commissioner
Tex Schramm — General manager

EQUIPMENT

The Field

The professional football field is 100 yards long and 160 feet wide, and the end zones are thirty feet deep. The goalposts are eighteen feet, six inches in width, and the top face of the crossbar must be ten feet above the ground. The vertical posts must extend at least thirty feet above the crossbar. The field is sometimes called a gridiron because the pattern of the lines resembles the cooking utensil used to broil foods.

The Ball

The football can weigh between fourteen and fifteen ounces. Its length can be from 11 to 11¼ inches. Its air pressure can be between 12½ and 13½ pounds per square inch.

Laces were used in early footballs to open the ball in order to insert or remove the rubber bladder holding the air. Today, laces remain because they provide a grip for holding and passing, even though there are no more ball bladders.

There are two theories about why the ball is so often called a "pigskin." Actually, footballs were never made of pigskin, but rather of steer or cow skin, with steer skin being more acceptable.

The first theory goes back to the eleventh century. A few years after the Danes left England in 1042, a farmer uncovered a skull and, guessing it was the skull of an enemy, began kicking it around. Other workers joined him and invented a game that might be called "skull-kicking." But since they wore sandals or soft-leather shoes, skull-kicking hurt their feet. Then someone replaced the skull with an animal bladder stuffed with straw. It might have been a pig's bladder, who knows?

The other theory says that at Rugby School in England, in order to make ball-carrying easier, the shape of the ball was changed from round to oval, and should be a "leather one, encased in a blown-up bladder." It might have been a pig's skin protecting a soft bladder.

The Uniforms

In the 1920s, the players had only one uniform, and laundry was a problem. Sometimes while on the road the players had to let the mud dry and then use a wire brush to clean their uniforms.

The strangest uniforms of all time were probably those of the 1934 Pittsburgh Pirates. The team wore horizontally-striped black and gold jerseys with matching socks. It was said that the team looked like a bunch of prison inmates.

The first leather helmets, called "head harnesses," were worn abut the turn of the century, but their main function was to protect the ears. In the 1930s, hard composition crowns were used in the helmets, and players immediately began to use the helmet as a weapon. In the late 1930s, plastic helmets were introduced and used throughout the 1940s. But there were a number of injuries caused by the plastic shattering, and leather and composition helmets were used during the 1950s until a new, stronger plastic shell was invented.

The Cleveland Browns are the only team not to have an insignia, or logo, on their helmets. Their helmets are a plain orange. The reason for this is that the Browns are the only team not to have an official emblem or logo.

The Cincinnati Bengals are the only team whose logo — tiger stripes — covers the entire helmet. In 1981, when the Bengals first came out with their tiger-striped helmets, they went 12-4 — the best record in the club's history.

The Pittsburgh Steelers have their emblem (the logo of United States Steel) only on the right side of their helmets — the only team to have it on just one side.

Football uniforms fit so tightly so that opposing players find it difficult to grab them when blocking or tackling.

In the early years, some NFL players used shin guards made of newspapers because their teams were having tough financial times.

The face mask was invented by coach Paul Brown of the Cleveland Browns in the 1950s.

The first player to wear a flak jacket was Houston Oilers quarterback Dan Pastorini. He had injured his ribs.

In 1973, the numbering system for the backs of jerseys was standardized. This is what the numbers mean.

1-19 — Quarterbacks and specialists

20-49— Running backs and defensive backs

50-59— Centers and linebackers

60-79— Defensive linemen and interior defensive linemen other than centers

80-89— Wide receivers and tight ends

90 and up — Defensive ends

The Arenas

In the early 1920s, the Providence (Rhode Island) Steam Roller played in the Cycledrome, which had been made for bicycle racing. It held 10,000 fans. There was only one locker room, built for bicycle teams of four. There were only two showers. Opponents had to dress at their hotel.

The first team to have wall-to-wall carpeting in its locker room was the Green Bay Packers under Coach Vince Lombardi.

Before D.C. Stadium (now RFK Stadium) was opened in 1961, the American Seating Company did a study that showed the average American's rear end was four inches wider than a century earlier. So seats were made twenty to twenty-two inches across instead of from seventeen to nineteen inches.

In 1966, the Houston Oilers refused to play in the brand-new Astrodome and chose Rice Stadium of Rice University instead. They finally moved to the Astrodome in 1968.

MONEY MATTERS

The Franchise

The lowest price ever paid for a franchise was one dollar for the Duluth Kelleys in 1926.

In 1925, Jimmy Conzelman bought the Chicago Cardinals for $40.

In 1933, the Philadelphia Eagles franchise was purchased for $2,500.

In 1933, the Pittsburgh franchise was bought for $2,500 by Art Rooney.

In 1938, the New York Giants made a profit of $200,000.

In 1941, the purchase price of the Cleveland Rams was $100,000.

In 1949, the Philadelphia Eagles were purchased for $250,000.

When the Baltimore Colts disbanded in 1951, the owner received $50,000 from the NFL for his players.

In 1953, the purchase price for the Cleveland Browns was $600,000.

When the Los Angeles Rams were sold in 1963, the price was $7,100,000.

In 1991, George Steinbrenner, the former managing partner of baseballs' New York Yankees, applied to purchase an expansion team in the Arena Football League. He paid $250,000 as a down payment on a team that would appear in 1993.

The Players

In 1938, the total payroll for all ten teams in the NFL was $560,000.

The salaries for 1920 ran about $50 to $75 a game, with the stars getting about $100.

By 1924, the wages had gone up some, with the average lineman getting $50-75 per game, the better linemen $100, the average backs $125-150, and the big stars $250-400. At that time, the maximum allowable payroll per game was $1,800.

Bronko Nagurski, the Hall of Fame back for the Chicago Bears, got $210.34 in extra pay for the Bears' victory in their first play-off championship in 1933. Thirty years later, in 1963, Larry Gluek got $5,899.77 for the same work when the Bears won the championship.

In the 1930s, Chicago Bears halfback Ray Nolting was paid $35 each time an ad for Bowman's Milk, in which he was the pitchman, appeared in one of the Chicago newspapers. He was allergic to milk.

Byron "Whizzer" White, the back of the Pittsburgh Pirates and future United States Supreme Court Associate Justice, was paid $15,800 for his rookie year in 1938.

After the 1940 championship game in which the Bears defeated the Redskins, each Chicago player received $873.99.

The next year, 1941, the winning Bears received only $430.94.

Although he was in the military service in 1945, Lou "The Toe" Groza was still paid $300 a week by the Browns.

Hall of Fame fullback Marion Motley of the Cleveland Browns was given a signing bonus of $100 in 1946.

In 1947, Charlie Trippi signed on as a back for the Chicago Cardinals for $100,000. This was the biggest salary since Red Grange signed with the Chicago Bears in 1925.

By 1948, the average annual salary in the NFL was about $6,000.

In 1950, the championship-winning Cleveland Browns each received $1,113.16 for the championship game.

By 1957, the NFL's minimum salary had risen to $5,000. That year the average salary on the Washington Redskins stood at $7,884. The highest total salaries were the Browns, and their players' salaries ranged from $6,000 to $19,000. Only four teams — the 49ers, Rams, Lions, and Chicago Cardinals had anyone making $20,000 or more.

In 1959, the Los Angeles Rams had the highest scouting costs in the NFL — $35,000.

Quarterback Joe Namath was signed as a rookie by the New York Jets in 1965. His three year contract called for a total salary of $427,000 — the most ever given to a collegian to turn pro at that time. In today's dollars, that is only $1.8 million for three years, and is not nearly what today's football stars earn.

In 1970, the minimum NFL salary had risen to $13,000. By far the highest paid NFL player was O.J. Simpson, the Buffalo Bills running back, at $806,668. The second highest paid player, Walter Payton, the running back of the Chicago Bears, was far down the scale at $450,000.

By 1988, the league's average salary was $230,000.

In 1990, the Indianapolis Colts drafted quarterback Jeff George and signed him for $15 million over six years. It was NFL's highest paid rookie contract in history.

The 1991 average salary was $422,149, and eighty-three players (twenty-nine of them quarterbacks) averaged $1 million or more. The average quarterback's salary stood at $856,000. Eighteen defensive linemen received more than $1 million.

In 1991, the Miami Dolphins signed quarterback Dan Marino to a five-year $25 million contract, making him the highest paid player in football history. At a press conference to announce the signing, Marino recalled that only ten years before he was making $10 an hour pouring concrete for a construction project at Pittsburgh's Three Rivers Stadium.

Miscellaneous Money

Football equipment was cheap in the 1909 catalogue of Sears, Roebuck & Company.

Victors Official Rugby Football — $3.20

Pebbled Leather Rugby Football — $1.50

Cowhide Rugby Football — $1.15

Grained Leather Rugby Football — .75

Worsted Football Jersey — $1.80

Cotton Football Jersey — .80

Twilled Football Jacket (with sleeves) — .50

Khaki Football Jacket (with sleeves) — .73

Twilled Football Jacket (sleeveless) — .37

Khaki Football Jacket (sleeveless) — .58

Twilled Football Pants — .58

Duck Football Pants — $1.00

Khaki Football Pants — $1.20

Rubber Nose Mask — .75

Football Mouthpiece — .10

Horsehide Football Helmet — $1.10

Here are some other prices and paychecks for various items and people.

1920 — League charter: $100

1920 — Blankets for the Rock Island Independents: $290

1923 — Chicago Bears program: 10 cents

1923 — Share of Green Bay Packers stock: $5

1926 — Hartford Blues season ticket: $17.25

1926 — Fine for breaking Canton Bulldogs training: $25

1929 — NFL bank balance in July: $1,960.05

1930 — Children's admission to Green Bay Packers games: 50 cents

1930 — Cost of padded jersey: $9.73

1933 — Winners' share in the first title game: $210.34

1933 — Officials' pay per game (paid by the home team): $25

1934 — Average player's salary per game: $110

1936 — Average guarantee for visiting team: $4,000

1957 — Cost of one Green Bay Packers Super Bowl ring: $2,600

1960 — Guarantee for visiting team: $40,000

1961 — Price of Minnesota Vikings season ticket: $40

1973 — Players' daily dinner allowance on the road: $9

1975 — Cost of the Louisiana Superdome: $175,000,000

1988 — Cost of average Phoenix Cardinals ticket: $38.56

1990 — Top pay per game for officials: $2,100

1991 — Top pay for Super Bowl officials: $8,500

In 1991, it was calculated that a family of four spends an average of $151.55 at an NFL game. That included four tickets, four hot dogs, four soft drinks, two beers, two souvenir caps, two programs, and parking. If the family goes to a San Francisco 49ers game, with the highest ticket price of $35, it would have to pay over $197.50. The best bargain in the league was a San Diego Chargers game, where it would cost $124.67.

MISCELLANEOUS TRIVIA

☞ The city flag of Green Bay, Wisconsin, features a wedge of cheese, a roll of paper, a ship, and a Packers helmet. After a Packers workout (usually attended by several hundred fans), the players head across the street to the stadium locker rooms, and an army of youngsters rushes up to volunteer the use of their bicycles to the players. The players ride off with the kids trotting alongside carrying the players' helmets.

☞ The first two Super Bowls were not called Super Bowls at the time. They were called AFL-NFL World Championship Games.

☞ As far as NFL statistics go, the farthest a ball can be run from scrimmage is ninety-nine yards.

☞ Most teams have an average of five men who scout the college players; the Cincinnati Bengals had only one in 1991.

☞ According to the *Encyclopedia of Sports Science and Medicine*, football is the most dangerous game in the world. The end run in football causes more injuries than any other play. Training exercises such as the full squat and the duck waddle are bad for the joints. If pep talks are legitimate to inspire athletes, so would be hypnosis.

☞ In the early 1920s, the Massillon (Ohio) Tigers once signed forty-five players for a game so that not a single good player would be left for the opposing team.

☞ According to an ad in 1923, the Hartford Fire Insurance Company was proud to insure all the Chicago Bears games against loss by rain, sleet, or snow.

☞ In 1928, two Green Bay Packers players, back Venne Lewellen and end Lavie Dilweg, ran for Green Bay district attorney. Lewellen, a Republican, won, but Dilweg was not even nominated by the Democratic Party.

☞ In 1934, with eleven teams in the league, the total attendance for the sixty games played in the NFL was a mere 492,684.

☞ The only doubleheader in NFL history occurred on August 25, 1939 in Green Bay. These were exhibition games with ten-minute quarters. The scores were Packers 7, Pittsburgh Pirates 7, and Packers 17, Pirates 0.

☞ In 1941, the Washington Redskins trained in San Diego, California, at Brown Military Academy. That is given the credit for making California become interested in professional football.

☞ On October 19, 1941, umpire C.W. "Chick" Rupp shot himself in the hand with his timer's gun in a game at the Polo Grounds between the New York Giants and Pittsburgh Steelers.

☞ In the first year for the Dallas Cowboys in 1960, they played in the Western Conference, but they were a "swing team," playing every other team in the league that year. They held their first training camp in Forest Grove, Oregon, quite a distance from Dallas.

☞ In 1961, hoping to sell out every home game, the Washington Redskins inaugurated the new D.C. Stadium (later RFK Stadium). But they drew only 37,767. Since 1966, however, they have sold out all their games.

☞ Appropriately, the New Orleans Saints were given their franchise on All Saints' Day, 1966.

☞ In 1970, an exhibition game of basketball was played between teams from the Houston Oilers and the Dallas Cowboys. Three players were ejected for fighting, and seventy fouls were called. The score was Houston 86, Dallas 84. Three Cowboys missed the next game — kicker Ron Widby (broken nose), back Walt Garrison (black eye), and end Dennis Homan (groin pull).

☞ In 1972, Robert Irsay bought the Los Angeles Rams for $19 million and traded the franchise to Carroll Rosenbloom for the Baltimore Colts.

☞ Kathy Shashaty, director of the Miami Dolphins cheerleaders, announced in 1991 that she was prohibiting her women from dating members of the team. At the time, two Dolphins, wide receiver Jim Jensen and defensive back Paul Lankford, were married to ex-cheerleaders.

☞ The Washington Redskins have a long waiting list for season tickets. In 1991, a writer for the *Baltimore Evening Sun* was notified that she could finally buy the seats she had asked for when she was a student at American University in Washington — after twenty-one years.

☞ For Super Bowl XXVI, bookies in Nevada and London came up with some rather strange bets that could be placed. Here are some of them, with the odds and the results.

American Odds

Washington wins, 10-0 (100-1) — Washington won, 37-24, you lose.

Buffalo wins, 24-21 (30-1) — Buffalo lost, 37-24, you lose.

At least one extra point is missed (3-1) — No extra points were missed, you lose.

Washington leads at the half, but loses the game (10-1) — Washington led at the half, but won the game, you lose.

Buffalo leads at the half, but loses the game (7-1) — Buffalo trailed at the half and lost the game, you lose.

Washington scores first on a touchdown pass (3-1) — Washington scored first, but on a field goal, you lose.

The first score is a Buffalo field goal (4-1) — The first score was a Washington field goal, you lose.

Quarterback Rypien throws more passes than quarterback Kelly (even) — Kelly threw 58, Rypien 21, you lose.

There will be ten or fewer total points (50-1) — There were sixty-one total points, you lose.

There will be ninety-one or more total points (20-1) — There were sixty-one total points, you lose.

British Odds

The first touchdown will be on a run by Thurman Thomas (6-1) — The first touchdown was on a pass by Rypien to Byner, you lose.

Rypien wins the most valuable player award (3-1) — He did, you win.

The third quarter will be the one in which the most points are scored (9-4) — It was, with twenty-four points, you win.

Norwood beats the Redskins on the last kick of the game, a field goal or an extra point (25-1) — Not in any way, you lose.

All in all, it doesn't pay to bet on football games.

10
What's in a Name?

One of the interesting things about football has been and always will be names and nicknames. Here are some of the best.

TEAMS

The Oorang Indians, who played in Marion, Ohio, were named after their owner's business. Walter Lingo owned the Oorang Kennels in LaRue, Ohio. He loved this breed of dog, which is a type of terrier.

The Decatur Staleys were named after the Staley Starch Company in Decatur, Illinois, and its owner, A.E. Staley.

When George Halas gained control over the Staleys and moved them to Chicago as the Chicago Staleys, he decided to change the name. He first thought of naming the team after the baseball team, the Chicago Cubs, but realized that Bears were more ferocious and bigger than Cubs.

The first owner of the Green Bay Packers was John Clair, who named them after his firm, the Indian Packing Company. He had put $500 toward the purchase of uniforms and equipment.

Although no real Vikings can be proven to have visited Minnesota, the name was adopted "due to historical ties believed to exist between the original Vikings and the area as well as the Nordic and Scandinavian ancestry of many in the area."

The New York Giants were named after the baseball team, which moved to San Francisco much later.

The Pittsburgh Steelers were named to represent the steel industry of the city.

The Philadelphia Eagles were named after the symbol of the National Recovery Act — a 1930s organization founded by President Franklin D. Roosevelt to ease the Great Depression — a blue eagle.

The Chicago Cardinals were named after the color of their uniforms — cardinal red. They had bought the suits from the University of Chicago, whose color was cardinal red.

The Kansas City Chiefs, Baltimore Colts, Seattle Seahawks, and Tampa Bay Buccaneers were all named after fan contests.

The Cleveland Browns were named after their coach, Paul Brown.

The Atlanta Falcons was suggested by schoolteacher Julia Elliott.

In the history of the NFL, four separate teams have been called the Bulldogs or Tigers. Three separate teams have been called the Maroons or Tornadoes.

NFL teams are named after animals, occupations, people, and things.

Animals

Bears	Eagles
Bengals	Falcons
Broncos	Lions
Cardinals	Rams
Colts	Seahawks
Dolphins	

Occupations

Buccaneers	Oilers
Chargers	Packers
Chiefs	Raiders
Cowboys	Steelers
49ers	

People

Browns (after coach Paul Brown)	Patriots
	Redskins
Bills (after Buffalo Bill Cody)	Saints
	Vikings

Things

Giants

Jets

Nicknames for Squads

The 1960s Rams defensive front — The Fearsome Foursome

The 1960s and 1970s Viking defensive unit — The Purple People Eaters

The 1970s Steelers defensive unit — The Steel Curtain

The Bills offensive line — The Electric Company

The Dallas defensive unit — The Doomsday Defense

The Broncos offensive unit — The Orange Crush

The Redskins offensive unit — The Hogs

STADIUMS

Sullivan Stadium, where the New England Patriots play, was named after William H. Sullivan, Jr., the first majority owner of the team.

San Diego Jack Murphy Stadium, where the San Diego Chargers play, was named after the late sports editor of the *San Diego Union.*

PLAYERS

Hall of Famer Green Bay Packers back, Johnny Blood, was born John McNally, but decided to change his name when he passed a movie theater advertising the film *Blood and Sand*, starring Rudolph Valentino.

From 1922 to 1923, the Oorang Indians of Marion, Ohio, sported the most oddly named lineup in league history. Among its players were Little Twig, Buffalo, Gray Horse, Long Time Sleep, Lone Wolf, Big Bear, Running Deer, Red Fox, Tomahawk, Woodchuck, Eagle Feather, Red Fang, Xavier Downing, and Laughing Gas.

He's Not Who You Think He Is
He's not the president or vice-president:

John Adams, Redskins tackle

John Adams, Bears back

William McKinley, Bills end

Henry Wallace, Los Angeles Chargers back

He's not the historical figure:

Samuel Adams, Patriots guard/tackle

John Brown, Los Angeles Dons center

John Brown, Browns/Steelers tackle

William Cody, Lions/Saints/Eagles linebacker

Charles Hugh, Eagles/Lions back/end

Thomas Hutchinson, Browns/Falcons end

Robert Kennedy, Los Angeles Dons back

Robert Lee, Patriots tackle

Robert Lee, Vikings/Falcons kicker

John Smith, Patriots kicker

John Smith, Eagles tackle

Joseph Smith, Colts end

He's not the writer:

Francis Bacon, Dayton Triangles back

Robert Browning, Kansas City Cowboys back

Robert Burns, Jets back

James Cain, Chicago Cardinals/Lions end

James Cain, St. Louis Cardinals end

Arthur Clark, Frankford Yellow Jackets/Duluth Eskimos back

James Cooper, Brooklyn Dodgers center

Ralph Emerson, Columbus Bullies guard

Arthur Haley, Canton Bulldogs/Akron Pros back

Samuel Johnson, 49ers/Vikings back

James Jones, Lions/Raiders back

James Jones, Jets/Redskins end

James Jones, Bears/Broncos end

John Leonard, Chicago Cardinals guard

Henry Miller, Brooklyn Dodgers back

Henry Miller, Detroit Heralds/Massillon Tigers/Buffalo All-Americans/ Frankford Yellow Jackets/Milwaukee Badgers end

John Milton, Kansas City Cowboys end

Drew Pearson, Cowboys end

James Riley, Dolphins end

Carl Sandberg, Minneapolis Redjackets back

He's not the musician:

Tony Bennett, Packers linebacker

James Brown, Browns back

John Cash, Broncos end

Andy Russell, Steelers linebacker

Robert Shaw, Rams/Chicago Cardinals end

John Williams, Eagles/Seahawks center

John Williams, Baltimore Colts/Rams tackle/guard

John Williams, Redskins/49ers back

He's not the actor:

William Boyd, Chicago Cardinals back

Frank Butler, Packers center

Art Carney, Giants guard

Gary Collins, Browns end/kicker

Robert Conrad, Chicago and St. Louis Cardinals/Cowboys back

Patrick Duffy, Dayton Triangles back

Richard Egan, Chicago Cardinals/Kenosha Maroons/Dayton Triangles end

Robert Hoskins, 49ers guard/tackle

Ronald Howard, Cowboys/Seahawks end

Buck Jones, Oorang Indians tackle

Robert Klein, Rams end

Jack Lord, Staten Island Stapletons guard

Robert Reed, Redskins guard
Robert Shaw, Saints end
Robert Young, Broncos/Oilers/St. Louis Cardinals guard/tackle

He's not the business tycoon:

Henry Ford, Browns/Steelers back
Joseph Kennedy, Buffalo Bisons back
Richard Sears, Kansas City Cowboys back

He's not the fictional character:

James Bond, Brooklyn Lions guard
Charlie Brown, Redskins wide receiver
Harold Hill, Brooklyn Dodgers end
Tom Jones, Minneapolis Redjackets guard
Tom Jones, Browns tackle
John Watson, 49ers tackle/guard

He's not the star in another sport:

Bill Bradley, Eagles back/kicker
Larry Brown, Redskins back
Jack Johnson, Bears/Bills/Dallas Texans back
John Henry Johnson, 49ers/Lions/Steelers/Oilers back
Walter Johnson, Browns tackle
John McKay, Buccaneers end
Ralph Sampson, Oilers tackle/end
John Sullivan, Buffalo All-Americans back

He's not the astronaut:

Neil Armstrong, Eagles end

Neat Nicknames
Animal Names

Lance "Bambi" Alworth, Chargers/Cowboys end
Alan "The Horse" Ameche, Baltimore Colts back
Walter "Piggy" Barnes, Eagles guard
Bob "Seabiscuit" Boyd, Rams end
Maurice "Mule" Bray, Pittsburgh Pirates tackle
Harlan "Whippet" Carr, Buffalo Bisons/Pottsville Maroons quarterback
Larry "The Atlantic City Airedale" Conover, Canton Bulldogs/Cleveland Bulldogs/Frankford Yellow Jackets center

Mike "The Animal" Curtis, Baltimore Colts/Seahawks linebacker

Grover "Ox" Emerson, Portsmouth Spartans/Lions/Brooklyn Dodgers guard

Gilbert "Hawk" Falcon, Hammond Pros/Chicago Tigers/Canton Bulldogs/ Toledo Maroons back

Austin "Goose" Gonsoulin, Broncos/49ers back

Casimir "Hippo" Gozdowski, Toledo Maroons back

Frank "Toadie" Greene, Chicago Cardinals back

George "Tiger" Greene, Falcons/Packers defensive back

Mike "Doggie" Gulian, Buffalo All-Americans/Frankford Yellow Jackets/ Providence Steam Roller tackle

Dean "The Tasmanian Devil" Hamel, Redskins/Cowboys defensive tackle

Ted "The Mad Stork" Hendricks, Baltimore Colts/Packers/Oakland Raiders linebacker

Jim "Turkey" Jones, Browns/Eagles/Browns end

Alex "The Mad Duck" Karras, Lions tackle

Herbert "Fido" Kempton, Canton Bulldogs back

Joe "Mink" Kresky, Boston Braves/Eagles/Pittsburgh Pirates guard

Ernie "Big Cat" Ladd, Chargers/Oilers/Chiefs tackle

Joe "Big Bird" Lavender, Eagles/Redskins back

Carl "Spider" Lockhart, Giants back

Gil "Wild Horse" Mains, Lions tackle

Ron "Dancing Bear" McDole, St. Louis Cardinals/Oilers/Bills end

Leo "The Lion" Nomellini, 49ers tackle

Stancil "Possum" Powell, Oorang Indians guard

Walter "Flea" Roberts, Browns/Saints/Redskins back/end

Noland "Super Gnat" Smith, Chiefs/49ers back/end

Ken "Snake" Stabler, Oakland Raiders quarterback

Clyde "Bulldog" Turner, Bears center

Charles "Pug" Vaughn, Lions/Chicago Cardinals back

Willie "Sugar Bear" Young, Bills/Dolphins tackle

Fast Nicknames

Roy "Bullet" Baker, New York Yankees/Packers/Chicago Cardinals/Staten Island Stapletons quarterback

Al "The Human Howitzer" Blozis, Giants tackle

Benny "The Purple Streak" Boynton, Rochester Jeffersons/Buffalo Bisons quarterback

Danny "Lightning" Butler, Steelers/Falcons/St. Louis Cardinals end

Jack "Flying" Cloud, Packers/Redskins back

Clyde "Cannonball" Crabtree, Frankford Yellow Jackets/Minneapolis Redjackets quarterback

Lamar "Racehorse" Davis, Miami Seahawks/Baltimore Colts end

Bill "Bullet Bill" Dudley, Steelers/Lions/Redskins back

Leslie "Speedy" Duncan, Chargers/Redskins back

L.G. "Long Gone" Dupre, Baltimore Colts/Cowboys back

Nello "Flash" Falaschi, Giants quarterback

Roy "Jet Stream" Green, St. Louis, Phoenix Cardinals wide receiver/defensive back

Arnie "Flash" Herber, Packers/Giants quarterback

Elroy "Crazylegs" Hirsch, Chicago Rockets/Rams end/back

Elvin "The Red Oak Express" Hutchinson, Lions back

Lionel "Little Train" James, Chargers wide receiver/halfback

Eddie "The Lawrence Flash" Kotal, Packers end

Dick "Night Train" Lane, Rams/Chicago Cardinals/Lions back

Joe "Midnight Express" Lillard, Chicago Cardinals back

Eugene "Mercury" Morris, Dolphins/Chargers back

John "The Diesel" Riggins, Redskins back

Frank "Slippery" Seeds, Canton Bulldogs back

Byron "Whizzer" White, Pittsburgh Pirates/Lions back

Food Nicknames

Jack "Butter" Fleischman, Detroit Panthers/Providence Steam Roller guard

Carlton "Cookie" Gilchrist, Bills/Broncos/Dolphins back

Max "Bananas" Krause, Giants/Redskins back

Romanus "Peaches" Madolney, Packers/Milwaukee Badgers guard

Edgar "Eggs" Manske, Eagles/Bears/Pittsburgh Pirates end

O.J. "Juice" Simpson, Bills back

Macho Nicknames

Dick "Bam Bam" Ambrose, Browns linebacker

Heartly "Hunk" Anderson, Bears guard

Bill "Knuckles" Boyle, Giants tackle

Bob "The Boomer" Brown, Lions/Rams tackle

Hardy "The Hatchet" Brown, Brooklyn Dodgers/Chicago Hornets/Baltimore Colts/Redskins/49ers/Chicago Cardinals/Broncos linebacker

Ross "Timber Beast" Carter, Chicago Cardinals guard

Guy "Champ" Chamberlin, Decatur, Chicago Staleys/Canton, Cleveland Bulldogs/Frankford Yellow Jackets/Chicago Cardinals end

Larry "Superman" Craig, Packers quarterback

Babe "Gunboat" Connaughton, Frankford Yellow Jackets guard

Sam "Bam" Cunningham, Patriots back

John "Jumbo" Elliot, Jets tackle/end

Bill "Earthquake" Enyart, Bills/Oakland Raiders back

Norman "Boomer" Esiason, Bengals quarterback

Frank "Gunner" Gatski, Browns/Lions center

Marshall "Biggie" Goldberg, Chicago Cardinals back

Clarence "Steamer" Horning, Detroit Heralds/Buffalo All-Americans/Rochester Jeffersons tackle

Gary "Big Hands" Johnson, Chargers tackle

Ed "Too Tall" Jones, Cowboys end

Eddie "King Kong" Kahn, Boston, Washington Redskins guard

Frank "Bucko" Kilroy, Steagles/Eagles tackle

Frank "Bruiser" Kinard, Brooklyn Dodgers/Brooklyn Yankees/New York Yankees tackle

Alphonse "Tuffy" Leemans, Giants back

Mike "Iron Mike" Mikulak, Chicago Cardinals back

Al "Old Pig Iron" Nesser, Akron Pros/Cleveland Bulldogs/Cleveland Panthers/Giants/Cleveland Indians guard

Sherman "Tank" Plunkett, Baltimore Colts/New York Titans/Jets tackle

Jack "Hacksaw" Reynolds, Rams linebacker

Al "Big 'Un" Rose, Providence Steam Roller/Packers/New York Yanks end

Ed "The Claw" Sprinkle, Bears end

Paul "Socko" Szakash, Lions back

Tom "The Bomb" Tracy, Lions/Steelers/Redskins back

John "Popeye" Wager, Portsmouth Spartans center

Arthur "Tarzan" White, Giants/Chicago Cardinals guard

Fred "The Hammer" Williamson, Steelers/Raiders/Chiefs back

John "Long John" Wilson, Cleveland Rams end

Tommy "Touchdown" Wilson, Rams/Browns/Vikings back

Casimir "Slug" Witucki, Redskins guard

Paul "Tank" Younger, Rams/Steelers back

Ugly Nicknames

Adrian "Barrel" Baril, Minneapolis Marines/Milwaukee Badgers tackle

Cliff "Gyp" Battles, Boston Braves/Boston, Washington Redskins back

William "Blink" Bedford, Rochester Jeffersons end

James "Goofy" Bowdoin, Packers/Giants/Brooklyn Dodgers/Portsmouth Spartans guard

Garland "Gob" Buckeye, Chicago Tigers/Chicago Cardinals/Chicago Bulls guard

Gil "Cactus Face" Duggan, Giants/Chicago Cardinals/Card-Pitts/Los Angeles Dons/Bills tackle

Glenn "Wackie" Frey, Eagles back

Earl "Jug" Girard, Packers/Lions/Steelers back

Joe "Mean Joe" Greene, Steelers tackle

Dick "Death" Halladay, Racine Legion end

Don "Jaws" Hardeman, Oilers back

Craig "Ironhead" Heyward, Saints back

Ernie "Fats" Holmes, Steelers tackle

Billy "Furnace Face" Kilmer, 49ers/Saints/Redskins quarterback

Fulton "Captain Crazy" Kuykendall, Falcons linebacker

Daryle "The Mad Bomber" Lamonica, Bills/Oakland Raiders quarterback

Howard "Fungy" Lebengood, Pottsville Maroons back

Carl "Moon Eyes" Littlefield, Cleveland Rams/Steelers/Buffalo Indians back

Russ "Cuss" Method, Duluth Kelleys, Eskimos/Chicago Cardinals back

Don "Dopey" Phelps, Browns back

Bucky "The Catawba Claw" Pope, Rams/Packers end

Elvin "Kink" Richards, Giants back

Joe "Muggsy" Sklaany, Eagles/Giants end

Hugh "Bones" Taylor, Redskins end

Bob "Old Stone Face" Waterfield, Cleveland, Los Angeles Rams quarterback

Herman "Squirmin' Herman" Wedemeyer, Los Angeles Dons/Baltimore Colts back

Norm "Wild Man" Willey, Eagles end

Dennis "Dirt" Winston, Steelers/Saints/Steelers linebacker

Elbert "Ickey" Woods, Bengals back

Women's Nicknames

John "Blondy" Black, Buffalo Bisons/Baltimore Colts back

Taldon "Tillie" Manton, Giants/Redskins/Brooklyn Dodgers back

Walter "Dainty" Moore, Pottsville Maroons back

Bill "Bubbles" Young, Giants tackle

Miscellaneous Nicknames

Walter "Sneeze" Achui, Dayton Triangles back

John "Tree" Adams, Redskins tackle

Ben "The Toeless Wonder" Agajanian, Steelers/Eagles/Los Angeles Dons/ Giants/Rams/Giants/Los Angeles Chargers/Dallas Texans/Packers/ Oakland Raiders/Chargers kicker

Ezzret "Sugarfoot" Anderson, Los Angeles Dons end

Reggie "Laughing Gas" Attache, Oorang Indians back

Howard "Screeno" Bailey, Eagles tackle

Leonard "Bear Tracks" Barnum, Giants/Eagles back

Ed "Bibbles" Bawel, Eagles back

Steve "Zeke" Bratkowski, Falcons/Redskins quarterback

Walter "Bubby" Brister, Steelers quarterback

Junious "Buck" Buchanan, Chiefs tackle

Tommonies "Mossy" Cade, Packers/St. Louis Cardinals defensive back

Tony "The Gray Ghost of Gonzaga" Canadeo, Packers back

Gino "The Duke" Capelletti, Boston Patriots end/kicker

Howard "Hopalong" Cassady, Lions/Browns/Eagles back

Johnny "Mr. Zero" Clement, Chicago Cardinals/Steelers/Chicago Hornets back

Merlin "The Magician" Condit, Steelers/Brooklyn Dodgers/Redskins/ Steelers back

Edward "Ty" Coon, Brooklyn Dodgers guard

Bob "Twenty Grand" Davis, Boston Yanks tackle

Len "Daddy Cool Breeze" Dawson, Steelers/Browns/Dallas Texans/Chiefs quarterback

Mark "Spoke" Devlin, Canton Bulldogs/Cleveland Panthers back

Enling "Dinger" Doane, Cleveland Indians/Cleveland Panthers/Milwaukee Badgers/Detroit Panthers/Pottsville Maroons/Providence Steam Roller back

Pat "Smoke Screen" Dowling, Chicago Cardinals end

Lyle "Hoot" Drury, Bears end

Francis "Jug" Earpe, Rock Island Independents/Packers/New York Yankees guard

Glen "Turk" Edwards, Steelers back/end

Alfred "Jitter" Fields, Saints/Colts/Chiefs defensive back

John "Frenchy" Fuqua, Giants/Steelers back

Howard "Hokie" Gajan, Saints/Chiefs back

Byron "Pills" Gentry, Los Angeles Bulldogs/Pittsburgh Pirates/Steelers guard

Bob "Harpo" Gladieux, Boston Patriots/Bills/Patriots back

Charles "Buckets" Goldenberg, Packers guard

Paul "Pitchin" Governali, Boston Yanks/Giants quarterback

Lou "The Toe" Groza, Browns tackle/kicker

Clarence "Dimp" Halloran, Hartford Blues back

Ken "One Round" Hauser, Buffalo Bisons/Newark Tornadoes back

Thomas "Hollywood" Henderson, Cowboys linebacker

Tony "Thrill" Hill, Cowboys wide receiver

Henry "Two Bits" Homan, Frankford Yellow Jackets quarterback

Paul "The Golden Boy" Hornung, Packers back

Henry "Honolulu" Hughes, Boston Braves back

Jack "Indian" Jacobs, Cleveland Rams/Redskins/Packers quarterback

Albert "Man O' War" Johnson, Brooklyn Dodgers/Bears/Chicago Cardinals/Eagles back

Billy "White Shoes" Johnson, Oilers wide receiver

David "Deacon" Jones, Rams/Chargers/Redskins end

Jim "Casey" Jones, Lions back

Tom "Emperor" Jones, Minneapolis Redjackets/Frankford Yellow Jackets/New York Yanks/Packers guard

Christian "Sonny" Jurgensen, Eagles/Redskins quarterback

Charley "Choo Choo" Justice, Redskins back

Mort "Devil May" Kaer, Frankford Yellow Jackets quarterback

George "Automatic" Karamatic, Redskins/Milwaukee Chiefs back

Harry "Jiggs" Kline, Giants end

Eugene "Big Daddy" Lipscomb, Rams/Baltimore Colts/Steelers tackle

Roy "Father" Lumpkins, Giants back

Kenneth "Kayo" Lunday, Giants center

Hugh "The King" McElhenny, 49ers/Vikings/Giants/Lions back

Gerald "The Ice Cube" McNeil, Browns/Oilers wide receiver

Don "Dandy Don" Meredith, Cowboys quarterback

Lyvonia "Stump" Mitchell, St. Louis, Phoenix Cardinals halfback

Lenny "Spats" Moore, Baltimore Colts back

Wilbur "Little Indian" Moore, Redskins back

Verne "Moon" Mullen, Evansville Crimson Giants/Canton Bulldogs/Bears/ Chicago Cardinals/Pottsville Maroons end

George "Sunny" Munday, Cleveland Indians/Giants/Cincinnati Reds/St. Louis Gunners/Brooklyn Tigers tackle

Jim "Sweet" Musick, Boston Braves/Boston Redskins back

Joe "Broadway Joe" Namath, Jets/Rams quarterback

Eddie "Five Yards" Novak, Rock Island Independents/Minneapolis Marines/Rock Island Independents back

Frank "Fudgehammer" Nunley, 49ers linebacker

Bill "Sidecar" O'Neill, Evansville Crimson Giants end

Clarence "Ace" Parker, Brooklyn Dodgers/Boston Yanks/New York Yankees quarterback

Walter "Sweetness" Payton, Bears back

William "The Refrigerator" Perry, Bears offensive tackle/offensive end/ back

Charles "Cotton" Price, Lions/Miami Seahawks quarterback

Abisha "Bosh" Pritchard, Cleveland Rams/Eagles/Giants back

Volney "Skeets" Quinlan, Rams/Browns back

Ulmo "Sonny" Randle, Chicago, St. Louis Cardinals/49ers/Cowboys end

Floyd "Breezy" Reid, Bears/Packers back

James "Tootie" Robbins, St. Louis, Phoenix Cardinals tackle

Bob "The Greek" St. Clair, 49ers tackle

Deion "Neon Deion" Sanders, Falcons defensive back

Clyde "Smackover" Scott, Eagles/Lions back

Charles "Bubba" Smith, Baltimore Colts/Oakland Raiders/Oilers end/ tackle

Julian "Sus" Spence, Chicago Cardinals/49ers/Oilers back

Roger "The Dodger" Staubach, Cowboys quarterback

Stewart "Smokey" Stover, Cowboys/Chiefs linebacker

Fred "Fuzzy" Thurston, Baltimore Colts/Packers guard

Jack "Baby Jack" Torrance, Bears tackle

Dan "Deacon" Towler, Rams back

Norm "The Dutchman" Van Brocklin, Rams/Eagles quarterback

Fred "Chopper" Vanzo, Lions/Chicago Cardinals quarterback

Dave "Nubbin" Ward, Boston Redskins tackle

Foster "Flippin" Watkins, Eagles back

Hodges "Burr" West, Eagles tackle

Wilbur "Wee Willie" Wilkin, Redskins/Chicago Rockets tackle

Jay "Inky" Williams, Canton Bulldogs/Hammond Pros/Kenosha Maroons/
Dayton Triangles/Cleveland Bulldogs end

Real Names that Sound Like Nicknames

Marger Apsit, Frankford Yellow Jackets/Brooklyn Dodgers/Packers/Boston Redskins back

Arrowhead, Oorang Indians end

J. Bourbon Bondurant, Muncie Flyers/Evansville Crimson Giants/Bears
guard

Eagle Day, Redskins quarterback

Xavier Downwind, Oorang Indians back

Jubilee Dunbar, Saints/Browns end

Fate Echols, St. Louis Cardinals/Eagles tackle

Nuu Faaola, Jets/Dolphins halfback/fullback

Sloko Gill, Lions guard

Fair Hooker, Browns end

Tunch Ilkin, Steelers tackle/guard/center

Honor Jackson, Patriots/Giants back

Proverb Jacobs, Eagles/Giants/New York Titans tackle

Wahoo McDaniel, Oilers/Broncos/Jets/Dolphins linebacker

Century Milstead, Giants/Philadelphia Quakers tackle

Golden Richards, Cowboys end

Prince Scott, Miami Seahawks end

Orenthal James Simpson, Bills back

Seaman Squyres, Cincinnati Reds back

Baptist Thunder, Oorang Indians guard

Yelberton A. Tittle, Baltimore Colts/49ers/Giants quarterback

Army Tomaini, Giants tackle

Zollie Toth, New York Yanks/Dallas Texans/Baltimore Colts back

Woodchuck Welmus, Oorang Indians end

11
Football in the Media

Football has never been the hottest subject in films or on television. In the movies, it has always taken a backseat to boxing and thoroughbred racing, and its appearance on TV is minuscule. But there are enjoyable films as well as literature on the subject of football. Here are some of them.

AT THE MOVIES

Professional football has given us many film actors — some good, some horrible. Here are several who have appeared in feature movies.

Sammy Baugh	Alex Karras
Jim Brown	Vince Lombardi
Roger Brown	Mike Lucci
Timmy Brown	Sid Luckman
Dick Butkus	John Matuszak
Paul Christman	Mike Mazurki
John Clement	Don Meredith
Larry Csonka	Joe Namath
"Boley" Dancewicz	Merlin Olsen
Paul Douglas	Joe Schmidt
Fred Dryer	O.J. Simpson
Bill Dudley	Bubba Smith
John Gordy	Woody Strode
Paul Governali	Pat Studstill
Red Grange	Charlie Trippi
"Mean Joe" Greene	Steve Van Buren
Elroy Hirsch	Bob Waterfield
Burl Ives	Guinn "Big Boy" Williams
"Indian Jack" Jacobs	Fred "The Hammer" Williamson

Early Films

Movies about football go back a long way. The first successful gridiron flick was probably *Brown at Harvard* (1921), which starred a largely forgotten Walter Haines, who was sometimes called "The Silent Clown." The movie can now be recalled by fewer people than attend a typical Brown-Harvard game.

But it was about college football, and for decades the usual football film was about college football. They were romantic and largely unbelievable, at least by modern standards. But they were made in a pre-television time when most people had never seen a college game, much less a professional game. After all, this was a time when professional football did not drag in the audiences that it does today.

Modern Films

It wasn't until the late 1960s that Hollywood thought of pro ball as being a usable topic for a movie. The time had come, probably because the American public was becoming aware of the professional game, and also because we were hearing more and more about the realistic side of the game — the off-the-field scandals, the greed, and the roughness. So, the audience was ready for more realistic fare, and the pros were the source of the realism, for the most part.

One of the early films was a most unusual movie — *Paper Lion* (1968). A writer named George Plimpton had written a book of the same name that described his experiences when he became an honorary member of the Detroit Lions football team and participated in preseason practice. He even ran a few plays at quarterback in an exhibition game. Starring Alan Alda (as Plimpton), Lauren Hutton, Alex Karras, and, in a small role, Roy Scheider, it was a movie that even non-football fans enjoyed, especially scenes that included Karras, who was a member of the team at the time. The real entertainment lay in the rich glimpse of training camp life.

Number One (1969) was a big disappointment for Charlton Heston fans. He played a quarterback for the New Orleans Saints who worries about getting too old to play anymore. It was an interesting idea but a bad film. Also starring were Jessica Walter and Bruce Dern.

Brian's Song (1971) was based on a true story about the deep friendship between two Chicago Bears running backs, the immortal Gale Sayers (played by Billy Dee Williams) and his roommate, Brian Piccolo (James Caan). Basically, the movie was about Piccolo's death from cancer in 1970. It was an unashamed real-life tearjerker — truly an exceptional film. Also in the cast were Jack Warden (as Bears owner-coach George Halas), Judy Pace, and Shelley Fabares. The movie won eleven awards.

Ben Johnson, the Academy Award winning actor, was the star of *Blood Sport* (1973). It told the story of a young boy who was being groomed by his father to become a professional football player. Johnson was the father, and the son was played by Gary Busey. Also in the cast were Larry Hagman and David Doyle. This satisfying film was an exceptional combination of character study and drama.

Burt Reynolds starred in *The Longest Yard* (1974), playing a former pro football player, Paul Crewe, who is serving time in prison for throwing games. (For a change of pace, Hollywood actually used an actor who had played football — Reynolds had been on the Florida State University team.) He is forced to form his own team of convicts ("The Mean Machine") to play Eddie Albert's handpicked team of prison guards. The Mean Machine finally won, 36-35. It was a hilarious bone-crunching comedy showing the variety of cheating that can go on in a football game. But some didn't like it. For example, the *Today* show's critic, Gene Shalit, said: "This movie should be penalized half the distance to the goal line — twice." But for the most part, it was an audience picture, and they loved it. Also in the cast were Ed Lauter, Michael Conrad, and Bernadette Peters.

Two Minute Warning (1976) featured Charlton Heston, John Cassavetes, Martin Balsam, Beau Bridges, David Janssen, Jack Klugman, and Gena Rowlands. It was pretty much a mess. The pointless story involved an attempt to catch a sniper in a packed football stadium. Audiences were tipped off that this was a contrived film with hackneyed characters when Merv Griffin appeared to sing the national anthem.

The next year, *Black Sunday* (1977) was released, and it was another "terror at the football game" movie. This time an international terrorist organization attempted to blow up the stadium during the Super Bowl. The movie was quite a few cuts above *Two Minute Warning*, and it was stolen by Bruce Dern as a crazed Vietnam veteran who pilots the television blimp. Also in the cast were Robert Shaw, Fritz Weaver, and William Daniels.

Semi-Tough (1977) starred Burt Reynolds (in another football movie) and Kris Kristofferson as two football stars who share an apartment and a girlfriend (Jill Clayburgh). Critics either loved it or they hated it. One writer, James R. Oestreich, called it a "... stinker ... Psychobabble is parodied heavy-handedly and at tedious length, all by crowding out the sport ... Evocative sloshing in Green Bay mud offers the only real diversion." On the other hand, many considered it an easy-going comedy in which Reynolds made up for the picture's deficiencies. Also in the cast were Robert Preston, Bert Convy, Lotte Lenya, and Brian Dennehy.

David Janssen, Edie Adams, Ken Howard, Van Johnson, Tom Selleck, Bubba Smith, and Dick Butkus starred in *Superdome* (1978). Taking a page from *Two Minute Warning*, this fly-by-night thriller told of a silent killer stalking New Orleans at Super Bowl time.

Heaven Can Wait (1978) was an amusing romp. Warren Beatty played a good-natured professional football player who is taken to heaven ahead of schedule and needs to return to "life" in another man's body in order to quarterback the Los Angeles Rams in the Super Bowl. Julie Christie was the love interest, and others in the cast were Buck Henry, Jack Warden, Dyan Cannon, Charles Grodin, James Mason, and Vincent Gardenia.

North Dallas 40 (1979) offered a fairly accurate and disturbing look at how the business side of professional football affects the player. It starred

Nick Nolte and Mac Davis, with Bo Svensen, Charles Durning, Steve Forrest, John Matuszak, and Dabney Coleman. Many critics thought that it was the best gridiron film ever made, and Nolte's depiction of bodily agony of defeat, and even of victory, was realistic enough to make any broken-down athlete cringe.

Robert Urich was the star of *Fighting Back* (1980). The film told the story of Rocky Bleier, the Vietnam hero turned Pittsburgh Steeler. (See Chapter 13.) Also in the cast were Art Carney, Bonnie Bedelia, Bubba Smith, and Howard Cosell.

FOOTBALL ON RADIO AND TELEVISION

As far as situation comedies are concerned, network television has never seen fit to explore the world of professional football. About as close as they ever came was to have Susan Saint James, the co-star of *McMillan and Wife* (a crime series of the 1970s) occasionally wear a football jersey bearing the number 18 in honor of Gene Washington, the stellar end of the San Francisco 49ers.

But when it comes to real-life programming, pro football has been powerful. In the 1970s, when he was coach of the New York Giants, Alex Webster was quite upset about his TV coverage. He threatened to sue Jim Bouton, who was doing sports for New York's WABC-TV, for $1,500,000 for running an interview of his on television without sound, making him look "like a dullard and a stupid person." The station claimed it was an accident, but Bouton remarked that he had really intended to run the interview backwards.

Television ratings are tremendous for Sunday games. Six of the top eleven highest-rated telecasts of all-time have been Super Bowls. Here's the rundown, with their years:

1. "M*A*S*H Special" 1983
2. "Dallas" 1980
3. *Roots*, part 8 1977
4. Super Bowl XIV 1980
5. Super Bowl XXVI 1992
6. Super Bowl XVII 1983
7. Super Bowl XX 1986
8. *Gone with the Wind* (part 1) 1976
9. *Gone with the Wind* (part 2) 1976
10. Super Bowl XII 1978
11. Super Bowl XIII 1979

In the Beginning

The first time anyone paid to sponsor professional football games on radio was in 1938. That was when General Mills paid a fee for the rights to NFL games. The price was a tiny $50,000.

The first NFL game ever to be televised was played on October 22, 1939, long before many people owned TV sets and a decade before the networks got into the action. It was a game at Brooklyn's Ebbets Field between the Philadelphia Eagles and the Brooklyn Dodgers, which ended in a 23-14 Dodgers victory. Most of the players didn't even know that they were being televised. The announcer was Allan "Skip" Walz, and only two cameras were used — one at ground level at the forty-yard line and one in the stadium balcony. There were no commercials, and it took only eight people to handle the telecast. Super Bowl games today use about 200 people.

By 1940, pro football had its first coast-to-coast radio broadcast. It was the championship game, and it was carried by 120 stations. The game was called by Red Barber. In 1946, the Chicago Bears got the first television paycheck — $5,400 for their six home games.

In 1950, the Los Angeles Rams were the first team to televise all their home games, at home and away. But in 1951 they stopped televising their home games after they lost more than $300,000 in gate receipts the year before.

In 1951, the championship game was televised coast to coast. The Rams beat the Browns, 24-7, at the Los Angeles Coliseum. That year, Commissioner Bert Bell made a policy of blacking out the city where the game was being played.

Pro Football Comes of Age on TV

Beginning in the 1950s, millions of people who had never seen a game in person now watched on television just at the time when football was being made even more exciting with explosive passing attacks by quarterbacks such as Otto Graham of the Browns, Bobby Layne of the Lions, and Johnny Unitas of the Baltimore Colts. The first coast-to-coast TV contract for a title game was signed by the NFL and the Dumont television network for $75,000, and CBS became the first network to televise regular season games — both in 1956. Still, in 1956, Frank Gifford, whose face would soon be familiar to millions as a TV football broadcaster, appeared on the TV game show *What's My Line*, in which a panel guessed what the guest did for a living. Gifford, the golden boy running back for the Giants, stumped the panel.

In 1958, the TV time-out raised its ugly head. It was, and is, a nonessential time-out to give the networks a chance to air still more commercials. Another innovation came in 1959, when CBS paid $3,000 to put a camera in the Goodyear Blimp. It took a while for an executive to be persuaded.

Prices went up in 1962 when the NFL entered into a single-network deal with CBS for $4.5 million. And in 1966 came the first Monday Night football game, but not on ABC. Frank Gifford and Lindsey Nelson called the game on October 31st for CBS. Pro football had become so popular on television that the 1967 championship game was carried by both CBS and NBC.

Then came "The Heidi Game" on November 17, 1968 between the New York Jets and the Oakland Raiders. The game was broadcast by NBC, and, with two minutes to go and the Jets ahead 32-29, the network switched to its regularly scheduled program, a made-for-TV version of the classic children's book, *Heidi*. In the last two minutes, unseen by anyone except the fans in the stadium, the Raiders scored twice to win 43-32.

In 1970 came the debut of ABC's Monday Night Football telecasts, handled by Howard Cosell, Don Meredith, and Keith Jackson. (Frank Gifford was to come later.) In addition to ABC on Monday, the NFL signed with CBS for NFC games and NBC for AFC games that year. And in 1975, the first woman debuted on football broadcasts. She was former Miss America Phyllis George, and she was the co-host of CBS' "NFL Today."

In 1980, ESPN was the first to televise the NFL draft. That same year came another first. NBC's sports executive Don Ohlmeyer aired an "announcerless" Jets-Dolphins game. No one said a word, but it wasn't necessary, since neither of the teams was going anywhere that year. It was a gimmicky way of experimenting with audio techniques before the upcoming Super Bowl game.

In 1985, hyping Super Bowl XX, NBC aired a "silent minute" in its pregame show. It was a gimmick for a bathroom break.

In 1986, instant replay was introduced. And in 1987, ESPN became the first cable network to air NFL games.

One last point. In the early days, radio and television broadcasters were men who knew how to communicate. They had spent years honing their craft. Today, every network color man for television games, plus some play-by-play announcers and studio hosts, is a former player or coach.

POETIC MUSINGS

The most successful author to come out of the NFL is Pete Gent, the former Cowboys flanker of the 1960s. His biggest triumph is the novel *North Dallas 40*, a romp about a professional football team. In the book are thinly disguised caricatures of Don Meredith, Tom Landry, and Tex Schramm, and it became a highly successful movie.

In November of 1985, a group of Chicago Bears players made a rap video, "Super Bowl Shuffle," even before they grabbed the prize. It outsold every video that year except Michael Jackson's "Thriller."

All in all, football men are not known as poets. An example of the typical doggerel coming from these men is the poem by Potsy Clark, who coached the Portsmouth Spartans. He handed out this to his players.

You strive until the goal is gained,
Then look for one still unattained.
Your record points the course you take,
To greater records you can make.
For hope springs not from what you've done,
But from the work you've just begun.

Finally, the honor of having the first team fight song in the NFL belongs to the Chicago Bears. Mercifully, the name of the lyricist has been forgotten. It isn't good poetry, but it is said that George Halas liked it. It was first sung in 1922.

From the East and from the West,
They send their very best
To play against the pride of old Chicago
There is none of them compare with our Chicago Bears.
Through the line they go.
Hold them down, Chicago, hold them down,
Is the cry of everybody in our town.
Just watch the way they meet and tumble their foe,
Out to win, Chicago Bears, they will always go.
Cross that line, Chicago, cross that line,
That's the way to play, you're doing fine,
And when the season's o'er and you have to play no more
Chicago Bears will stand out force.

12
Odds and Ends

73-0

The Championship game in 1940 between the Chicago Bears and the Washington Redskins, played in Washington, was a historic one. Years later, when George Halas, the owner-coach of the Bears, was asked what his greatest thrill in his long career had been, he smiled and said "73-0." There was no doubt what he meant. Professional athletic scores are usually forgotten the day after the game, but this one lives on.

The most fantastic exhibition of sheer football power and genius, combined with perfect timing and good luck, made this championship game into one that will be mentioned with awe as long as football is played. Washington was far from an outclassed team. In fact, their season record (9-2) was better than the Bears' (8-3). The Redskins were expected to win, especially since "Slingin' Sammy" Baugh, their quarterback, was having his best year ever.

The Bears received the opening kickoff, and on the second play fullback Bill Osmanski sped around his left end for sixty-eight yards and a touchdown. Halfback Jack Manders converted. Sid Luckman, the Bears quarterback, scored the next touchdown with a one-yard plunge after driving the team eighty yards. Second-string quarterback Bob Snyder kicked the extra point. Halfback Joe Maniaci followed Osmanski's trail around left end for forty-two yards and a touchdown, and guard Phil Martinovich made the conversion to make it 21-0 at the end of the first quarter.

The second quarter was fairly quiet. The only scoring was Luckman's thirty-yard pass to end Ken Cavanaugh in the end zone and Snyder's second conversion.

End Hampton Pool intercepted a Sammy Baugh pass to open the second half and ran nineteen yards for a touchdown, with end Dick Plasman converting. Halfback Ray Nolting blasted for twenty-three yards and another score, but this time Plasman missed the conversion. Halfback George McAfee then intercepted substitute quarterback Roy Zimmerman's pass and returned it thirty-four yards for a touchdown; tackle Joe Stydahar kicked the extra point. Center Clyde "Bulldog" Turner got into the act by intercepting another Zimmerman pass and going twenty-one yards into the end zone. The Redskins blocked Maniaci's conversion attempt, and this made it 54-0 as the third quarter ended.

Halfback Harry Clark went around his right end for forty-four yards and a touchdown, but Gary Famiglietti missed the conversion. A few minutes later, Famiglietti atoned for his fluff by smashing over from the two-yard line after Turner had recovered substitute quarterback Frankie Filchock's fumble. This time, Bears substitute quarterback Sollie Sherman passed to Maniaci for the extra point. Clark scored the final touchdown from the one-yard line, but the Sherman-Maniaci conversion pass went wild. The reason that the Bears passed instead of kicked for the conversions late in the game was that they were running out of footballs because so many had been kicked into the stands and not returned. At the end of the game, the two teams were using an old practice football. Ten different Bears had scored eleven touchdowns, and six different Bears had scored seven conversions in this 73-0 rout — the worst beating in NFL history.

SNEAKERS, ANYONE?

In 1934, the Chicago Bears won the Western Division championship with their 13-0 perfect record. But the New York Giants barely edged out the Boston Redskins in the Eastern Division with an 8-5 mark. Obviously, the Bears were heavily favored, but no one had counted on the miserable weather in New York for the championship game at the Polo Grounds.

The temperature was nine degrees at kickoff time, and the field was covered with a sheet of ice. The first quarter of this slipping and sliding game ended 3-0 for the Giants after a field goal by fullback Ken Strong. But, in the second quarter, the Bears came back, scoring a touchdown on a one-yard rush by fullback Bronko Nagurski, a conversion by halfback Jack Manders, and a field goal by Manders. At the half the score was Bears 10, Giants 3.

But a trainer for the Giants had been busy. What the Giants needed were sneakers instead of their regular football shoes. That should make them more sure-footed on the ice. Somehow he was able to borrow the sneakers from the Manhattan College gymnasium, and the New Yorkers donned them during the halftime break.

Manders kicked another field goal in the third quarter. But then the roof starting falling in on the Bears. It was obvious in the fourth quarter that the Giants were getting used to their new footwear.

The final period started off with a touchdown — a twenty-eight-yarder from quarterback Ed Danowski to end Ike Franklin, with a point after touchdown by Strong. Then Strong galloped forty-two yards for another score and kicked his own conversion. Strong came back to score again on an eleven-yard rush, but missed the extra point. Danowski, not to be outdone, ran the ball in from six yards out, and Strong kicked another point-after to run his personal total for the day to eighteen points. The game ended with the sneaker-shod Giants triumphing, 30-13.

NAMATH'S GUARANTEE

No one did more to give the Super Bowl its magic than New York Jets quarterback Joe Namath. Super Bowl III, Namath's Super Bowl, will always be remembered. Going into the championship game, the Baltimore Colts, with their 13-1 mark, were heavily favored over the Jets (11-3).

On the Thursday before the game, Namath told a gathering at the Miami Touchdown Club banquet: "We're going to win Sunday, I'll guarantee you." When questioned after the banquet, he added, "We're a better team than Baltimore."

His remarks irritated coach Weeb Ewbank of the Jets, whose team was rated as the underdog by seventeen to nineteen points. He moaned to Namath, "Ah, Joe, Joe. You know what they're gonna do? They're gonna put that on the locker room wall. Those Colts are gonna want to kill us."

Namath, unabashed, answered him: "Well, Coach, you've been telling us for the last two weeks that we're gonna win, right? I just let the rest of the people know what you've been thinking. Coach, don't you think we're gonna win?"

The first quarter was scoreless, with each team feeling out the other. But in the second quarter, running back Matt Snell of the Jets ran the ball in from the four and kicker Jim Turner converted. The Jets were off to the races.

Turner kicked two field goals in the third quarter, and the score was 13-0. He kicked another in the fourth quarter to make the score 16-0. By this time it was obvious that the Colts were overconfident and flat. They had gone into scoring territory five times and came out scoreless each time. Not until late in the last quarter did fullback Jerry Hill score on a one-yard rush, with kicker Lou Michaels converting.

For the first time, an American Football League team had won the Super Bowl. It was the Jets, 16-7. Ironically, the flamboyant Namath had beaten the Colts that day with a conservative approach. His longest pass was thirty-nine yards, and he moved the Jets in methodical fashion.

After the win, he trotted off the field, his right index finger pointed to the sky. For his leadership as well as his quarterbacking, he was named the game's most valuable player.

THE IMMACULATE RECEPTION

December 23, 1972 was the day of the AFC play-off game between the Pittsburgh Steelers and the Oakland Raiders. The score stood at 7-6 in favor of the Raiders, with only twenty-two seconds left. The Steelers had the ball, but it was fourth and ten, and they were on their own forty-yard line. Obviously, a pass play was coming, and Oakland organized a heavy blitz.

As quarterback Terry Bradshaw faded back, he saw that his primary receiver, wide receiver Barry Pearson, was covered. While scrambling, Bradshaw found his man — halfback Frenchy Fuqua — and threw the pass.

But Fuqua and Oakland safety Jack Tatum smashed into each other, and the ball was deflected by Tatum into the air. Suddenly, from out of nowhere, came rookie fullback Franco Harris. Harris later said, "When the play got messed up, I was running toward Fuqua, hoping he'd get the ball and I could block for him." Instead, Harris found the ball heading his way. He scooped it up at full stride, just above the grass. He raced down the left side of the field and scored. The game ended at 13-7 after the conversion. So miraculous was the play that it became known as the immaculate reception.

THE FIRST HALL OF FAMER

The man who was named the greatest athlete and football player of the first half of the twentieth century was born in Prague, Oklahoma, on the Sac and Fox Indian Territory, on May 28, 1888. A Native American, his Indian name was Bright Path.

Already a great athlete, he went to the Carlisle Indian School in Pennsylvania, where he played football under the legendary coach, Pop Warner (after whom the Pop Warner Boys' football program was named). Among the teams he helped defeat were Harvard and Army. Indeed, Thorpe had some of the responsibility for making future President Dwight D. Eisenhower give up playing football. Eisenhower of the Army team wrenched his knee while trying to tackle Thorpe.

Thorpe was off to Europe in 1912 to appear in the Stockholm, Sweden, Olympic Games. On the ship bound for Sweden, it is said that he would climb to the ship's upper deck and search for the iceberg that had sunk the ocean liner *Titanic* several months earlier.

He was the star of the Olympics. He won both the pentathlon (with four of five first places) and the decathlon (with 8,412.96 points out of a possible 10,000). But disappointment was to follow.

Thorpe had been paid for playing baseball for both Rocky Mount and Fayetteville of the Eastern Carolina minor league (1909-10) and that meant he was not an amateur athlete. His Olympic records were nullified, and his medals were taken away. The medals were not returned until 1982, twenty-nine years after his death.

Thorpe went on to play baseball for the New York Giants, Cincinnati Reds, and Boston Braves. But when he returned to playing football, he became a star. This first president of the American Professional Football Association (later the NFL) played for the Canton Bulldogs (1919-20), the Cleveland Indians (1921), the Oorang Indians (1922-23), the Toledo Maroons (1923), the Rock Island Independents (1923), the New York Giants (1925), and the Bulldogs again (1926).

In 1963, Jim Thorpe became the very first man to be elected to the Pro Football Hall of Fame.

PAPA BEAR

"Papa Bear," "Mr. National Football League" — those two nicknames were often used to refer to Chicago Bears player-owner-coach George Staley Halas. Born in Chicago on February 2, 1895, Halas found himself off to the Navy in 1917. World War I was beginning for the United States, and he had finished his football playing days at the University of Illinois. He had also been a star in baseball (the New York Yankees wanted him) and basketball (he was team captain in his senior year).

But when he arrived at the Great Lakes Naval Training Station in Illinois, he found that they played football, too. He played end for the team and assisted in wins over the Naval Academy at Annapolis and many other fine college teams. Great Lakes also tied Notre Dame and played in the 1919 Rose Bowl Game.

Discharged as a naval ensign, he reported to the Yankees at spring training. He was doing rather well, but then he met A.E. Staley, the owner of a corn products company in Decatur, Illinois. Staley want to organize a football team, and he wanted Halas to play for him. When the American Professional Football Association was organized, Halas was there. The first year, with Halas as player-manager, the Decatur Staleys were 5-1-2, and Papa Bear was on his way.

For the next five decades, the Decatur, Chicago Staleys/Chicago Bears dominated professional football. They won the most championships (seven); they won the most games (over 400); they scored the most points (more than 11,000); they gained the most yards (nearly twenty-five miles); they scored the most touchdowns (nearly 1,600); they played to the most fans (nearly 15,000,000); they made the most money. And they were penalized the most.

Halas instilled team spirit, and the Bears often won games with inferior teams because of this spirit. But Halas retired as a player in 1932, or as he said, "When they began to run over me, under me, around me, and through me." He stayed on as coach for many years, with time off to serve as a naval commander during World War II.

Halas was first in many things. The Chicago Staleys were the first official champions of the league in 1921. They were the first professional team to have daily practices. They were the first to travel coast-to-coast. They were the first to have their games broadcast on radio. They were the first to use game films for analysis. They were the first to use the man-in-motion off the T formation.

George Halas built a team and founded a dynasty of sport. He gave the Bears quality, spirit, and dramatic ability. The National Football League can be credited to him more than any other man.

Halas was elected to the Pro Football Hall of Fame in 1963. He died on October 31, 1983, never knowing that his beloved Bears would win Super Bowl XX, beating the Patriots 46-19, at the time the widest margin ever in a Super Bowl.

NUMBER 77

When he was starring for the University of Illinois football team, Harold "Red" Grange was the subject of an exchange between rival Big Ten coaches. "All Grange can do is run," said Fielding Yost, football coach at the University of Michigan. To which the University of Illinois mentor, Bob Zuppke, replied, "All Galli-Curci [the world-famous coloratura soprano of the 1920s] can do is sing."

Born June 13, 1903 in Forksville, Pennsylvania, Grange early on moved with his family to Wheaton, Illinois. He was to become the sports idol of his age. With his flaming hair and his many notable achievements on the football field — some so spectacular that they still read like fiction — Red Grange fit easily into that group of superstars who helped elevate the 1920s into the golden age of sports in the United States. It was a group that included baseball player Babe Ruth, tennis star Bill Tilden, swimmer and actor Johnny Weissmuller, boxer Jack Dempsey, and golfer Bobby Jones.

His legend began as a running back on the University of Illinois team in 1924. In his first game, he ran thirty-five yards for a touchdown against the University of Nebraska — in the first quarter! Then, in the second quarter, came a sixty-five-yard touchdown run. And in the final quarter there was another touchdown, this time for twelve yards.

In his first Big Ten game, against the University of Iowa, he caught three passes on a drive that took Illinois to the two-yard line. He then went in for the score, and Illinois had beaten Iowa for the first time in twenty-two games.

Then Illinois faced the undefeated University of Michigan team. That day was also the dedication day for Illinois' new Memorial Stadium, and 66,609 people turned out for the game. Grange took the opening kickoff ninety-five yards for a touchdown. Then, on Illinois' next possession, he took a hand-off for a sixty-seven-yard touchdown. Later came touchdown runs of fifty-four and forty-four yards. He had run for 265 yards and scored four touchdowns in the first twelve minutes of the game. Grange then took a breather, but came back to score his fifth touchdown of the day on a sixteen-yard run. For good measure, he threw a twenty-yard scoring pass in the fourth quarter as Illinois won 39-14. In forty-one minutes of play, he was responsible for 402 yards of offense, including sixty-four yards as a passer.

For his performance that day, and for the rest of the season, sportswriter Damon Runyon wrote of him: "He is three or four men rolled into one. He is Jack Dempsey, Babe Ruth, Al Jolson, Paavo Nurmi, and Man o' War."

Grange ended his collegiate career with a total of 2,071 yards rushing over three seasons. His rushing average was 5.3 yards per carry. He had scored thirty-one touchdowns and thrown six scoring passes. The great sportswriter Grantland Rice was the one who coined the nickname for Grange of the "Galloping Ghost." (He was also known as the "Wheaton Iceman" for a summer job he had held.) The nickname was so widely known that Grange later made a series of cliffhanger movie serials called *The Galloping Ghost.*

In November 1925, Grange was ready for a new adventure. It was he who was to change the professional game from a sport that drew tiny crowds to a sport that made the front pages. George Halas, the player-owner-coach of the Chicago Bears, signed Grange to a professional contract — effective immediately.

On Thanksgiving Day, Grange joined the team to begin a tour that helped lift pro football into the American consciousness. He started for the Bears on November 26th and collected $12,000. But he was worth it. He pulled 36,000 fans in for his first game in Cubs Park (later to become Wrigley Field), when the Bears played the Chicago Cardinals. The next week, he drew 28,000 spectators for a game against the Columbus Tigers. Later, 66,000 fans came to see him play the Giants at the Polo Grounds in New York.

Three months after his debut, he and the Bears had finished a barnstorming tour that included games in New York, Providence, Washington, Pittsburgh, Detroit, Tampa, Jacksonville, Miami, New Orleans, Los Angeles, San Diego, San Francisco, Portland, and Seattle. By now, Grange had earned $100,000.

Then, in 1926, Grange formed his own team in the new American Football League — the New York Yankees. In 1927, the AFL having collapsed, he took his Yankees to the NFL. After that season, the Yankees were disbanded, and Grange went back to the Bears, where he starred until 1934.

After a brief career as an assistant coach, he left the game to try a number of pursuits, including acting. He returned to football as an announcer and analyst on radio and television, broadcasting many college games and 312 Bears games from 1947 to 1961.

Grange died on January 28, 1991, in Lake Wales, Florida. Once he was asked for his fondest football memory. Grange did not refer to his heroics as a running back. He recalled a game against the University of Iowa when Earl Britton, his prime blocker on runs, kicked a fifty-five-yard field goal. Red explained, "I held the ball for him."

DOUBLE-BARRELED FOOTBALL MEN

There have been quite a few football celebrities who also starred in other sports. Here are some of them.

Basketball

Some players played both professional football and professional basketball in the same years. When they played, what was to become the National Basketball Association was hurting and wages were low. So the basketball pro teams were only too happy to arrange a special contract for big name players, who would report whenever they were finished with football that year. Here are some:

Dick Evans: Green Bay Packers; Sheboygan (Wisconsin) Redskins

Len Ford: Cleveland Browns; Dayton (Ohio) Rens

Ted Fritsch: Green Bay Packers; Oshkosh (Wisconsin) All-Stars

Otto Graham: Cleveland Browns; Rochester (New York) Royals

Bud Grant: Philadelphia Eagles; Minneapolis (Minnesota) Lakers

Vern Huffman: Detroit Lions; Indianapolis (Indiana) Kautskys

Connie Mack Berry: Chicago Bears; Oshkosh (Wisconsin) All-Stars

Otto Schnellbacher: New York Giants; St. Louis (Missouri) Bombers

Bob Shaw: Cleveland Rams; Youngstown (Ohio) Bears

Clint Wager: Chicago Cardinals; Oshkosh (Wisconsin) All-Stars

Ron Widby: Dallas Cowboys; New Orleans (Louisiana) Buccaneers

Lonnie Wright: Denver Broncos; Denver (Colorado) Rockets

Baseball

Some football superstars were also baseball superstars. One of the earliest was Ernie Nevers, who became a Hall of Famer for his play for the Duluth Eskimos and the Chicago Cardinals. He also played baseball with the old St. Louis Browns of the American League. Bo Jackson, a halfback with the Los Angeles Raiders, has played baseball for the Kansas City Royals and the Chicago White Sox. He was the first athlete to be named to the all-star team in both sports. Unfortunately, after a hip injury in 1991 during a Raider's play-off game, it is not known if Bo Jackson will ever play professional sports again.

But the football/baseball star who has caught the imagination of all sports fans today is "Neon Deion" Sanders. He leans toward football with the Atlanta Falcons, but he also plays for the Atlanta Braves. Here is an example of what he went through in 1991.

Sanders, one of the few people in history to play both major league football and major league baseball, left the Atlanta Braves in 1991 when the Atlanta Falcons started training camp. In the fourth game of the football season, on September 21st, the Falcons had defeated the Los Angeles Raiders, 21-17. Sanders, a defensive back, had been named the defensive player of the week in the NFL for that game.

But then came an urgent request from the Braves, who were in the thick of the National League West baseball pennant race. The Braves had just lost their leadoff man, Otis Nixon, who was leading the major leagues in base-stealing with sixty, and they needed some help from the fleet-footed Sanders.

He spent the morning of September 25th at football practice. He went through calisthenics, catching drills, and pass coverage drills. Then he showered and went to a Falcons team meeting. Usually he would go home after all this and take a nap. But not this time.

After the team meeting broke up, Sanders boarded a news helicopter from an Atlanta television station and sailed southward to downtown Atlanta, where he landed in a parking lot near the State Capitol.

"It was real fast," he said. "I've never ridden in a helicopter before and it was something else."

Once Sanders touched down, a television station car took him to the ballpark, where he arrived wearing a sweatsuit and carrying a football. He was finally available for a baseball game on the same day he had practiced with his football team. In the first game of a doubleheader with the Cincinnati Reds, Sanders was inserted at first as a pinch runner, and promptly stole second base.

Sanders' Falcon football coach, Jerry Glanville, took it all in stride. "As long as he gets his work done here, which he is ... If he can go help them, it's fantastic."

Two Other Nuggets

Walt Garrison, while he was a running back with the Dallas Cowboys, was also a rodeo rider.

Joe Gibbs, the Washington Redskins coach, has a stock car team in the NASCAR Winston Cup circuit.

FOOTBALL'S BIG BUCKS

Professional football has come a long way since players were lucky if they made $100 per game. For example, quarterback John Elway of the Denver Broncos, who began his career in 1983, will have earned about $17.7 million at the end of his first ten years in the league. Compare that with the payment due for the two new 1976 franchises in the NFL — the Seattle Seahawks and Tampa Bay Buccaneers — only $16 million each.

And here are the eleven top quarterback salaries in the NFL for the 1991 season.

1.	Dan Marino	Miami Dolphins	$4.433 million
2.	Joe Montana	San Francisco 49ers	$3.25
3.	Boomer Esiason	Cincinnati Bengals	$3.0
4.	Jim Kelly	Buffalo Bills	$2.864
5.	Warren Moon	Houston Oilers	$2.833
6.	Randall Cunningham	Philadelphia Eagles	$2.563
7.	Jeff George	Indianapolis Colts	$2.5
8.	Jim Everett	Los Angeles Rams	$2.4
9.	Bernie Kosar	Cleveland Browns	$2.329
10.	Steve Young	San Francisco 49ers	$2.24
11.	John Elway	Denver Broncos	$1.957

13
Men of Courage

Over the years, there have been countless football players who demonstrated more courage than the average person can comprehend. Hundreds of players have overcome bigotry, poor health, and physical handicaps. They are inspirations to us all.

BLACKS IN FOOTBALL

In the early days, black football players were not completely shut out. Indeed, long before the American Professional Football League was formed, there were several pro players who were black. Perhaps the first was Charles Follis, who played for the Shelby (Ohio) Athletic Club team from 1902 to 1906.

Some of the other black stars were:

Paul Robeson (also a great singer): Hammond Pros (1920)/Akron Pros (1921)/Milwaukee Badgers (1922), linebacker

Fred "Duke" Slater: Milwaukee Badgers (1922)/Rock Island Independents (1922-25)/Chicago Cardinals (1926-31), tackle

John Shelbourn: Hammond Pros (1922), halfback

Frederick "Fritz" Pollard: Akron Pros (1919-21, 1925-26)/Milwaukee Badgers (1922)/Hammond Pros (1923-25)/Providence Steam Roller (1925), running back

But after the formation of the APFA (later the NFL), only thirteen black men played during the years from 1920 to 1932. The last were Chicago Cardinals back Joe Lillard and Pittsburgh Pirates tackle Ray Kemp. Before the 1933 season came the infamous unwritten "gentleman's agreement" to ban black players. And this was to last until 1945.

Finally, in 1946, blacks began to appear in the NFL and the All-American Conference. Kenny Washington was signed by the Los Angeles Rams, as was Woody Strode (who went on to become a fine actor). The Cleveland Browns of the AAFC signed fullback Marion Motley and guard Bill Willis.

It took until 1948 before the first black players appeared on football cards. They were Kenny Washington and Detroit Lions end Bob Mann. In 1949, the NFL still had only five blacks, but the AAFC had eleven, although they had three fewer clubs in their league.

By 1950, there were eighteen blacks in the NFL, but that represented only four percent of the players in the league. The Bears put the first black quarterback on the field in 1953 — Willie Thrower. By 1959, there were fifty-two blacks in the league, representing 11.5 percent of the players.

In 1962, the last NFL team to have an all-white lineup, the Washington Redskins, broke the color barrier by drafting running back Ernie Davis. They traded him to the Cleveland Browns for black receiver Bobby Mitchell. The next year, 1963, Emlen Tunnell of the Giants became the first black assistant coach, and, in 1965, field judge Burl Tolar became the first black NFL official.

The first black referee in the NFL, Johnny Grier, took the field in 1988. That was the same year in which the first black quarterback started in the Super Bowl. He was Doug Williams of the Washington Redskins.

At last, a black man became coach of an NFL team in 1989 — Art Shell of the Los Angeles Raiders. He was to be followed by Dennis Green of the Minnesota Vikings in 1991.

Today, the whole question about being a black player is summed up by Randall Cunningham, star quarterback of the Philadelphia Eagles. When he was asked by a reporter about how he felt being a black quarterback in Philadelphia, he answered directly. "Am I supposed to be a white quarterback? A Chicano quarterback? Well, you know I'm a South Philadelphian. I thought I was Italian."

Later he said, "I'm just me. I'm a black person. I'm a football player. I don't play for a black football team. I go out and play football. This is a sport. It doesn't matter what color you are."

WORLD WAR II

As far as courage is concerned, take a look at the NFL's record in World War II. Going into service were 638 employees of the league, and sixty-nine earned military decorations. Two ends — John Lummus of the New York Giants and Maurice Britt of the Detroit Lions — were awarded the Congressional Medal of Honor, the United States' highest decoration for bravery. Lummus was killed while leading a platoon on Iwo Jima, and Britt lost an arm while fighting in Italy.

ROCKY BLEIER

Today he is a rare man. Rocky Bleier runs a successful motivational speaking business, and he has four Super Bowl rings and a Purple Heart. After a fine career at the University of Notre Dame, he had played one year at halfback for the Pittsburgh Steelers before he was drafted into military service in 1968. Then he was off to Vietnam.

While on patrol in the Que San Valley in August 1969, this Wisconsin native was shot in the left leg by a sniper. Soon after, a Vietcong grenade exploded just six feet away. Bleier's legs were ripped by shrapnel, and his right foot was mangled. After he was evacuated, Army doctors declared him forty percent disabled and said he would never play football again. But Bleier was sure that he would return to the NFL.

"I never had another dream," he recalled. "I just wanted to come back and play pro football. I knew I didn't want to end up being forty years old and wondering whether I could've made it back."

Bleier spent months rehabilitating his injured legs and foot, and fought his way back to the Steelers in 1971. While helping Pittsburgh win four Super Bowls, the five-foot, eleven-inch back gained 4,659 yards and the admiration of millions. In 1974, he earned the Halas award, which goes to professional football's most courageous player.

BO JACKSON

His future was probably the brightest in all sports. Bo Jackson was named the winner of the Bert Bell Memorial Trophy in 1987 — given to the outstanding rookie in the NFL. Jackson had been a standout player at Auburn University and had been the first-round draft pick at halfback by the Tampa Bay Buccaneers in 1986. He also was a baseball star, playing for the Kansas City Royals.

It was estimated in 1990 that Jackson would earn about $1,480,000 from his new football team, the Los Angeles Raiders; $1,000,000 from the Royals; and $5,000,000 in endorsements. His "Bo Knows" ads for Nike's cross-trainer shoes caused a doubling of their sales in 1989. Jackson also worked for Salem Sportswear (T-shirts), Costacos Brothers Sports (posters), Pepsi-Cola, AT&T, General Mills, and Cramer Products (Bo Med sports medicine equipment). He was named the most successful athlete in selling products on television.

He worked hard on the non-profit side, too. He had done anti-drug and stay-in-school TV promotionals, and was involved with the Marillac Foundation in Kansas City for emotionally disturbed children.

Jackson's football record was stellar. He was voted to the NFL's Pro Bowl. (And he also played in baseball's All-Star Game.) Then he smashed his left hip in a play-off game in January 1991. Doctors advised him not to return to football, and the Royals gave up on him, trading him away to the Chicago White Sox.

What might have happened if his football career had continued is stunning. He had played thirty-eight games for the Raiders when he injured his hip. This can be compared to the first thirty-eight games of the great Hall of Famer of the Chicago Bears, Gale Sayers.

	Jackson	Sayers
Attempts	515	535
Yards gained	2,782	2,725
Average yards per attempt	5.4	5.2
Touchdowns	16	27

Put another way, in terms of records per game:

	Jackson	Sayers
Attempts	13.6	14.1
Yards	73.2	71.7
Average	5.4	5.1
Touchdowns	.4	.7

In the summer of 1991, Jackson failed his football physical, and it was rumored that he would never play the game again. But he kept on working, and the White Sox did not give up on him.

In his first seventeen games as a designated hitter for Chicago in 1991, he hit .260 with three home runs and thirteen runs batted in. That is hardly the record of a man with no future.

According to the White Sox trainer, Herman Schneider: "The hip will get stronger. I don't have any doubt about that. The problem will always be there, but he can overcome it by strength and work. He'll always have a little bit of a limp; that's to be expected from now on. His left leg is a little shorter than the right because he lost cartilage. But a lot of guys play without cartilage."

In March of 1992, the White Sox put Jackson on waivers, not so much to get rid of him, but rather to re-sign him to a new contract without exercising his $91,000 option. That same month, the superstar decided to have a hip replacement. On April 4th, surgeons gave him his new artificial hip, and perhaps there was hope that he could make a comeback.

JOE NAMATH

Hall of Fame New York Jets quarterback Joe Namath has badly damaged knees that date back to his playing days at the University of Alabama. Yet he enjoyed a stellar career, both in college and in the pros. After seven operations on his knees, in constant pain, he was forced to retire in 1978 at the age of thirty-four.

With his constant pain and with his arthritic condition worsening, Namath was forced once again to go for surgery. In 1992, he underwent a four-hour operation to replace both of his knees.

TOM DEMPSEY

It was November 8, 1970. The Detroit Lions were playing the New Orleans Saints. With only a few seconds left to go in the game, the Saints had the ball in their own end of the field and were trailing by one point. Having no confidence in a "Hail Mary" pass, and knowing that they had only one play to go, they called in their field goal kicker and hoped for a miracle.

Tom Dempsey was not what you would think of as a miracle worker. He was a product of tiny Palomar College (a junior college) in San Marcos,

California, and this was but his second season in the NFL. He was a little man. And add to the fact that he had physical problems. He was born with a withered right arm that ended in only two fingers and no hand. He was also born without toes on his right foot (his kicking foot). His right foot was size 3, and his shoe was padded. Still, he never seemed to realize he was handicapped.

Dempsey stepped into the ball and kicked an incredible sixty-three-yard field goal. This bettered the previous record that had stood for seventeen years — fifty-six yards. He also beat the Lions on the last play of the game, 19-17.

Later, one of the finest tributes to this man was uttered by Alex Karras, the former Outland Award-winning tackle from the University of Iowa, who was playing as a defensive lineman for the Lions that day. "... the most exciting game that I was ever in was one that we lost. New Orleans had a player by the name of Tom Dempsey who was handicapped from birth. He had a withered arm and a club foot. We were leading the Saints with about a half minute to go. New Orleans had the ball, but not in scoring position. In came Dempsey, who proceeded to kick a National Football League record-breaking sixty-three-yard field goal. That beat us, but I'll never forget my admiration for that man."

14
Other Leagues

Over the years, there have been many professional leagues that rose to challenge the dominance of the National Football League. Still others have played in peaceful coexistence with the NFL.

FORGOTTEN TEAMS

Many teams have disappeared when their leagues disappeared. Here are some who were in the American Football League I (1926), the American Football League II (1936-37), the American Football League III (1940-41), the All-America Football Conference (1946-49), the American Football League IV (1960-69), the World Football League (1974-75), and the United States Football League (1983-85).

Alabama
Birmingham
Americans, 1974 (WFL)
Vulcans, 1974 (WFL)
Stallions, 1983-85 (USFL)

Arizona
Phoenix
Arizona Wranglers, 1983-85 (USFL)

California
Anaheim
Southern California Sun, 1974-75 (WFL)

Los Angeles
Wildcats, 1926 (AFL I)
Bulldogs, 1937 (AFL II)
Dons, 1946-49 (AAFC)
Chargers, 1960 (AFL IV)
Express, 1983-85 (USFL)

Oakland
Invaders, 1983-85 (USFL)

Colorado
Denver
Gold, 1983-85 (USFL)

District of Columbia
Washington
Federals, 1983-84 (USFL)

Florida
Jacksonville
Sharks, 1974 (WFL)
Express, 1975 (WFL)
Bulls, 1984-85 (USFL)

Miami
Seahawks, 1946 (AAFC)

Orlando
Florida Blazers, 1974 (WFL)
Renegades, 1985 (USFL)

Tampa
Tampa Bay Bandits, 1983-85 (USFL)

Hawaii
Honolulu
Hawaiians, 1974-75 (WFL)

Illinois
Chicago
Bulls, 1926 (AFL I)
Rockets, 1946-48 (AAFC)
Hornets, 1949 (AAFC)

Fire, 1974 (WFL)
Blitz, 1983-84 (USFL)

Louisiana
New Orleans
Breakers, 1984 (USFL)

Shreveport
Steamer, 1974-75 (WFL)

Maryland
Baltimore
Stars, 1985 (USFL)

Massachusetts
Boston
Shamrocks, 1936-37 (AFL II)
Bears, 1940 (AFL III)
Breakers, 1983 (USFL)

Michigan
Detroit
Wheels, 1974 (WFL)
Michigan Panthers, 1983-84
  (USFL)

New Jersey
East Rutherford
New Jersey Generals, 1983-85
  (USFL)

Newark
Bears, 1926 (AFL I)

New York
Brooklyn
Horsemen, 1926 (AFL I)
Tigers, 1936 (AFL II)
Dodgers, 1946-48 (AAFC)

Buffalo
Indians, 1940-41 (AFL III)
Bisons, 1946 (AAFC)

New York
Yankees, 1926 (AFL I)
Yankees, 1936-37 (AFL II)
Yankees, 1940 (AFL III)
Americans, 1941 (AFL III)
Yankees, 1946-49 (AAFC)
Titans, 1960-62 (AFL IV)
Stars, 1974 (WFL)

Rochester
Tigers, 1936-37 (AFL II)

North Carolina
Charlotte
Hornets, 1974-75 (WFL)

Ohio
Cincinnati
Bengals, 1937 (AFL II)
Bengals, 1940-41 (AFL III)

Cleveland
Panthers, 1926 (AFL I)

Columbus
Bullies, 1940-41 (AFL III)

Oklahoma
Tulsa
Oklahoma Outlaws, 1984 (USFL)

Oregon
Portland
Storm, 1974 (WFL)
Thunder, 1975 (WFL)
Breakers, 1985 (USFL)

Pennsylvania
Philadelphia
Quakers, 1926 (AFL I)
Bell, 1974-75 (WFL)
Stars, 1983-84 (USFL)

Pittsburgh
Americans, 1936-37 (AFL II)
Maulers, 1984 (USFL)

Tennessee
Memphis
Southmen, 1974-75 (WFL)
Showboats, 1984-85 (USFL)

Texas
Dallas
Texans, 1960-62 (AFL IV)

Houston
Texans, 1974 (WFL)
Gamblers, 1984-85 (USFL)

San Antonio
Wings, 1975 (WFL)
Gunslingers, 1984-85 (USFL)

Wisconsin
Milwaukee
Chiefs, 1940-41 (AFL II)

CANADIAN FOOTBALL LEAGUE

The Canadian Football League goes back a long way. What is now the Eastern Division began competition in 1892. In 1936, teams in the West were added, forming another division. Teams have come and gone, but today the CFL consists of eight teams.

Eastern Division	Western Division
Hamilton Tiger-Cats	British Columbia Lions
Ottawa Rough Riders	Calgary Stampeders
Toronto Argonauts	Edmonton Eskimos
Winnipeg Blue Bombers	Saskatchewan Roughriders

The Canadian game is played on a field 160 yards long and 65 yards wide. Another important difference between American and Canadian football is that each team fields twelve men in Canada. On offense, this twelfth man usually lines up in the backfield, but he may also be used as an end. On defense, he usually plays in the secondary.

There are several differences in the rules, too.

1   The offense has only three downs to make a first down.

2.   There is a "dead-line" twenty-three yards behind each goal line. On a kickoff, the receiving team must advance the ball out of the area between the dead-line and the goal line. If it fails, the kicking team scores one point, called a "single." The same rule applies to a punt.

3.   Any number of backfield players can be in motion in any direction at the snap.

4.   A point after touchdown counts one point if kicked or two points if it is the result of a run or a completed pass into the end zone.

5.   If a punted ball travels through the end zone and across the dead-line, it counts one point, called a "rouge" or a single.

6.   A fair catch is not allowed on a punt, but tacklers must stay five yards away from the receiver until he has touched the ball.

7.   On punt returns, blocking above the waist is permitted.

8.   After a field goal, the team scored against may take a first down, kick off from its thirty-five-yard line, or elect to receive a kickoff.

9.   After a rouge, the team scored against gets a first down on its thirty-five-yard line.

10.   Only one time-out is allowed each team per half, and only in the last three minutes of that half.

The Grey Cup is awarded annually to the CFL championship team. In 1909, Earl Grey, the governor-general of Canada, donated the trophy for the Rugby Football championship of Canada. Since 1954 it has been given to the professional football top team. Here are the winners and losers of the championship games.

1954 — Edmonton Eskimos 26, Montreal Alouettes 25

1955 — Edmonton Eskimos 34, Montreal Alouettes 19

1956 — Edmonton Eskimos 50, Montreal Alouettes 27

1957 — Hamilton Tiger-Cats 32, Winnipeg Blue Bombers 7

1958 — Winnipeg Blue Bombers 35, Hamilton Tiger-Cats 28

1959 — Winnipeg Blue Bombers 21, Hamilton Tiger-Cats 7

1960 — Ottawa Rough Riders 16, Edmonton Eskimos 6

1961 — Winnipeg Blue Bombers 21, Hamilton Tiger-Cats 14

1962 — Winnipeg Blue Bombers 28, Hamilton Tiger-Cats 27

1963 — Hamilton Tiger-Cats 21, British Columbia Lions 10

1964 — British Columbia Lions 34, Hamilton Tiger-Cats 24

1965 — Hamilton Tiger-Cats 22, Winnipeg Blue Bombers 16

1966 — Saskatchewan Roughriders 29, Ottawa Rough Riders 14

1967 — Hamilton Tiger-Cats 24, Saskatchewan Roughriders 1

1968 — Ottawa Rough Riders 24, Calgary Stampeders 21

1969 — Ottawa Rough Riders 29, Saskatchewan Roughriders 11

1970 — Montreal Alouettes 23, Calgary Stampeders 10

1971 — Calgary Stampeders 14, Toronto Argonauts 11

1972 — Hamilton Tiger-Cats 13, Saskatchewan Roughriders 10

1973 — Ottawa Rough Riders 22, Edmonton Eskimos 18

1974 — Montreal Alouettes 20, Edmonton Eskimos 7

1975 — Edmonton Eskimos 9, Montreal Alouettes 8

1976 — Ottawa Rough Riders 23, Saskatchewan Roughriders 20

1977 — Montreal Alouettes 41, Edmonton Eskimos 6

1978 — Edmonton Eskimos 20, Montreal Alouettes 13

1979 — Edmonton Eskimos 17, Montreal Alouettes 9

1980 — Edmonton Eskimos 48, Hamilton Tiger-Cats 10

1981 — Edmonton Eskimos 26, Ottawa Rough Riders 23

1982 — Edmonton Eskimos 32, Toronto Argonauts 16

1983 — Toronto Argonauts 18, British Columbia Lions 17

1984 — Winnipeg Blue Bombers 47, Hamilton Tiger-Cats 17

1985 — British Columbia Lions 37, Hamilton Tiger-Cats 24

1986 — Hamilton Tiger-Cats 39, Edmonton Eskimos 15
1987 — Edmonton Eskimos 38, Toronto Argonauts 36
1988 — Winnipeg Blue Bombers 22, British Columbia Lions 21
1989 — Saskatchewan Roughriders 43, Hamilton Tiger-Cats 40
1990 — Winnipeg Blue Bombers 50, Edmonton Eskimos 11
1991 — Toronto Argonauts 36, Calgary Stampeders 21

AMERICAN FOOTBALL LEAGUE (NUMBER 1)

C.C. "Cash and Carry" Pyle was a promoter who was also Harold "Red" Grange's manager. It was his idea to organize a league to take on the NFL — the American Football League. Grange had led the Chicago Bears on that 1925 coast-to-coast tour, and had proved he had great drawing power. So Pyle put together a New York team, the Yankees, with Grange as the star, and came up with a nine-team league. The members were:

Boston Bulldogs

New York Yankees

Brooklyn Horsemen

Newark Bears

Chicago Bulls

Philadelphia Quakers

Cleveland Panthers

Rock Island Independents

Los Angeles Wildcats

Just because there was a team called the Los Angeles Wildcats didn't mean that professional football had come to the West Coast. It was a team without a home field and played all its games east of the Mississippi River. The teams had a good supply of the top professional players of the time, but not all the franchises finished the season.

The championship of the league was won by the Philadelphia Quakers, with their 7-2-0 record. The Yankees, with Grange, were second, with a 9-5-0 record.

The league disbanded after that one season, but Grange and his Yankees joined the NFL, playing in that league for two more years. Other AFL players were picked up by NFL teams. Finally, Grange went back with the Bears in 1928, playing with them through 1934.

AMERICAN FOOTBALL LEAGUE (NUMBER 2)

Another American Football League appeared in 1936. Some of its teams lasted two years, the life span of the league as a whole. Here were the teams for those two brief years:

Boston Shamrocks (1936-37)

Cincinnati Bengals (1937)

Brooklyn Tigers (1936)

Cleveland Rams (1936)

Los Angeles Bulldogs (1937)

New York Yankees (1936-37)

Pittsburgh Americans (1936-37)

Rochester Tigers (1936-37)

Syracuse Braves (1936)

The Rochester Tigers did not begin the 1936 season. Actually, the team was a merger of the Syracuse Braves and the Brooklyn Tigers early in 1936.

As far as championships go, there were some problems. In 1936, the Boston Shamrocks were the champions, since they had the best record. But the championship game between Boston and Cleveland was canceled because the Shamrock players had not been paid for several games.

In 1937, there was no doubt. The new Los Angeles Bulldogs had gone through their entire season undefeated.

AMERICAN FOOTBALL LEAGUE (NUMBER 3)

Still another AFL was organized in 1940, and people began to wonder why they couldn't come up with a new, or at least luckier, name. This league also lasted but two years, despite the fact that it was able to gather some top-level players.

In 1940, the final standings looked like this:

Columbus Bullies	8-1-1
Milwaukee Chiefs	7-2-0
Boston Bears	7-2-0
New York Yankees	4-5-0
Buffalo Indians	2-8-0
Cincinnati Bengals	1-7-0

In 1941, Boston had dropped out of the league, and New York and Buffalo had changed their names. The final standings were these:

Columbus Bullies	5-1-2
New York Americans	5-2-1
Milwaukee Chiefs	4-3-1
Buffalo Tigers	2-6-0
Cincinnati Bengals	1-5-2

The Bullies had won both championships. The Bengals had been able to manage only two wins. The league went out of business.

ALL-AMERICA FOOTBALL CONFERENCE

Finally, a new league with some pizzazz appeared in 1946. It was the All-America Football Conference, and it had been founded by Arch Ward, sports editor of the *Chicago Tribune*, who had also been responsible for the baseball All-Star Game and the football College All-Star Game.

More successful than the previous maverick leagues, it started with eight teams:

Brooklyn Dodgers	Los Angeles Dons
Buffalo Bills	Miami Seahawks
Chicago Rockets	New York Yankees
Cleveland Browns	San Francisco 49ers

The Brooklyn Dodgers had been in the NFL, but their owner, Dan Topping, took them to the new league. The Cleveland Browns took over the vacant spot created in that city by the Cleveland Rams' move to Los Angeles the previous fall.

After the first season, Miami dropped out and was replaced by the Baltimore Colts.

In the last year of the league, 1949, Brooklyn merged with the New York Yankees, and Chicago changed its name from the Rockets to the Hornets. In 1950, three of the teams were given NFL franchises — the Cleveland Browns, Baltimore Colts, and San Francisco 49ers.

In the All-America Football Conference, the Cleveland Browns were phenomenal. Under the leadership of future Hall of Famers coach Paul Brown and quarterback Otto Graham, and featuring future Hall of Fame fullback Marion Motley and pass catcher Dante Lavelli, they won the league championship every year the conference was in existence.

In fifty-four regular-season games, they lost only four times and were tied only three times. In 1948, they were undefeated. After they joined the NFL, they continued to demonstrate their class, winning six division championships in a row, 1950-1955.

AMERICAN FOOTBALL LEAGUE (NUMBER 4)

In 1960, the last American Football League (to date, anyway) was formed. But this one was not destined for failure because of money problems, since it, like the NFL, had a generous television contract.

The league began with eight teams:

Eastern Division	**Western Division**
Boston Patriots	Dallas Texans
Buffalo Bills	Denver Broncos
Houston Oilers	Los Angeles Chargers
New York Titans	Oakland Raiders

Over the next few years, there were some changes, of course. The Dallas Texans became the Kansas City Chiefs in 1963. The Chargers moved from Los Angeles to San Diego in 1961. The New York Titans became the Jets in 1963.

The games in this league seemed to be a bit more exciting, since the teams stressed the passing game and had a rule that a touchdown conversion could count two points if it were run in or a completed pass.

The NFL and the AFL battled it out for several years for television and stadium viewers and college talent. The AFL even tried to sign up NFL stars.

The AFL-NFL war reached its peak in 1966, with the two leagues spending a combined total of $7 million to sign their draft choices that year. But it was too much, and, in 1966, the two leagues agreed to merge. They would play separate schedules until 1970, but meet in a world championship game beginning in 1967. Thus the National Football Conference and the American Football Conference were born. To balance things out, the Pittsburgh Steelers, Baltimore Colts, and Cleveland Browns agreed to go to the AFC.

WORLD FOOTBALL LEAGUE

The World Football League began play in 1974, but it didn't last long. The first twelve franchises were:

Western Division
Honolulu Hawaiians
Houston Texans
Portland Storm
Southern California Sun

Central Division
Birmingham Americans
Chicago Fire
Detroit Wheels
Memphis Southmen

Eastern Division
Florida Blazers
Jacksonville Sharks
New York Stars
Philadelphia Bell

From the beginning, the league was a mess. Originally, there was to be a team in Toronto, and all-pros like Larry Csonka, Jim Kiick, and Paul Warfield of the Miami Dolphins were signed to play in Canada. But restrictions imposed by the Canadian government forced the team to move to Memphis before the start of the season. Then it turned out that these three, plus many other NFL stars, were already signed by their NFL teams for the 1974 season, and could not join their new teams until the next year.

Also, the league padded attendance figures, missed payrolls, shifted franchises (the Charlotte Hornets, Shreveport Steamer, and San Antonio Wings later made their appearance), and lost uniforms and equipment because of confiscation for bad debts. The Detroit Wheels actually had to borrow athletic tape from another team and the players had to bring their own towels to games. The league lost about $20 million. It was an embarrassment.

When the 1975 season started, Detroit and Florida had been dropped, and all but two clubs (Memphis and Philadelphia) were under new management. But without a television contract, the league died a quiet death on October 22, 1975, just past the halfway mark of the season.

Just for the record, the only title game, in 1974, drew only 32,376 fans. Birmingham beat Florida, 22-21.

UNITED STATES FOOTBALL LEAGUE

The United States Football League began playing in 1983. It began as a spring football league, playing an eighteen-week schedule from March through June — normally football's off season. But the public wasn't ready for spring football. The original lineup looked like this:

Atlantic Division
Boston Breakers
New Jersey Generals
Philadelphia Stars
Washington Federals

Central Division
Birmingham Stallions
Chicago Blitz
Michigan Panthers
Tampa Bay Bandits

Pacific Division
Arizona Wranglers
Denver Gold
Los Angeles Express
Oakland Invaders

Teams dropped out and teams dropped in. Among the newcomers were:

Pittsburgh Maulers
New Orleans Breakers
Memphis Showboats
Jacksonville Bulls
Houston Gamblers
San Antonio Gunslingers

Oklahoma Outlaws
Baltimore Stars
Orlando Renegades
Arizona Outlaws
Portland Breakers

It obviously was not a stable league, but it played three championship games.

1983 — Michigan Panthers 24, Philadelphia Stars 22
1984 — Philadelphia Stars 23, Arizona Outlaws 3
1985 — Baltimore Stars 28, Oakland Invaders 24

The league died after its third season, in 1985.

WORLD LEAGUE OF AMERICAN FOOTBALL

A new league with a few important differences was the World League of American Football, which debuted in 1991. To begin with, its teams were not only North American teams, but European teams as well. Then, too, the NFL was backing the operation. It was hoped that the new league would serve as a sort of minor league operation — funnelling the best players into the NFL. Only the Chicago Bears and Phoenix Cardinals refused to give money to the league.

There were to be some new rules in the league, which played its games in the spring. A thirty-second play clock was instituted, a team could go for a two-point conversion, and in overtime a team had to win by at least nine points. Kicks had to be brought out of the end zone.

The twenty-six supporting NFL teams had to put up $50,000 each and then set up a line of credit — but they would get a percentage of the profits, if any. The league got a $24 million deal for four years with ABC and a $26 million contract for two years from the USA cable network. All this money was not going to the players, however. The average salary in the first years was $40,000, including ten games and play-off games. But some of the top players made $100,000.

The first game in the WLAF, which by now had been called "The Laugh League," was played on March 23, 1991. The London (England) Monarchs beat the Frankfurt (Germany) Galaxy, 24-11. Just two days before the first game in Barcelona, Spain, the goalposts were still not in the ground at Montjuic Olympic Stadium. They had been held up in Spanish customs, as was most of the equipment shipped from the United States. When holes were dug for the goalposts, one of them filled with water. Then the posts were planted in concrete.

The games were a little informal. At halftime some of the fans could be invited onto the field to dance with the cheerleaders. The New York/New Jersey Knights offered a two-for-one ticket deal on the side of a milk carton. After the games, players shook hands with their opponents. The league even tried putting cameras in the helmets of quarterbacks to show the home television audience charging linebackers. There were fire-eaters in Birmingham at Fires games. The Montreal Machine fans were mechanics' uniforms to games. Sacramento Surge fans wore green surgeons' smocks and called themselves "The Surge on Generals."

The WLAF spent $500,000 to publicize the first championship game — the World Bowl '91. The game was won by the London Monarchs, who beat the Barcelona Dragons 21-0. The music on the field was provided by the maroon-and-gold uniformed Central State Invincible Marching Marauder Band and Belles from Wilberforce, Ohio. The attendance was an amazing 61,108.

But after its first year, the league had lost $7 million. The television ratings in the United States were half those expected. And in Europe, broadcasts by Eurosports, a London cable network broadcasting to twenty-one other countries, were not financial bonanzas.

It was estimated that it would cost between $600,000 and $700,000 to keep the league in operation for the second year. After all, none of the teams had made money. One NFL owner said, "It's a financial sinkhole, and we're throwing good money after bad." But Paris was applying for a franchise as were Amsterdam, Bogota, Tel Aviv, Lithuania, and Moscow.

The WLAF learned its fate at a meeting of NFL owners in Dallas. In October 1991, the owners voted to continue the league. In 1992, play began for the second year, with the following teams on the field:

North American West
Birmingham (Alabama) Fire
Sacramento (California) Surge
San Antonio (Texas) Riders

North American East
Montreal (Canada) Machine
New York/New Jersey Knights
Ohio (Columbus) Glory
Orlando (Florida) Thunder

European Division
Barcelona (Spain) Dragons
Frankfurt (Germany) Galaxy
London (England) Monarchs

The Ohio Glory replaced the Raleigh-Durham (North Carolina) Skyhawks of the year before. And Sacramento beat Orlando, 21-17, in the World Bowl in Montreal before 43,759 fans.

SOME VARIATIONS

Arena Football

The Arena Football League began in 1987. Arena football is not a miniature version of the NFL game. It is a violent sandlot game played indoors. The field is only fifty yards long, so an offensive team is almost always in scoring position and almost all plays are passes. The players make about $5,000 a season — they are usually good college athletes who failed to make the NFL. Most of them go both ways, playing on offense and defense. There are eight franchises, and the league hopes to expand. In 1991, the Tampa Bay Storm beat the Detroit Drive, 48-42 in the Fifth Arena Bowl '91.

Russian Football

The U.S.S.R. Association of American Football began in 1990. At the end of its second season, it was time for Moscow's first "Super Bowl of American Football." The two best teams in the six-team league faced each other on September 29, 1991 in Moscow's Locomotive Stadium. The Moscow Swans played the Moscow Bears, and huge Soviet athletes dressed in shoulder pads and jerseys were selling tickets before the game at ten rubles apiece (about five dollars).

Boris Zaichuk, the Swans' coach, told of his training. "We have been learning from video cassettes and books by [Vince] Lombardi."

On the artificial turf of Dynamo Stadium, the Swans were practicing, wearing their black helmets on which were painted the head and curling neck of a swan. The quarterback, Andrei Isaev, crouched behind his center and barked, "myach!," which is Russian for "ball!" Fading back, he pumped-faked and handed off to Alek Sedotov, who sprinted off-tackle for five yards. "O.K., O.K.," yelled Zaichuk. "Just like the 49ers."

Pop Warner Football

Pop Warner Football is a national organization that charters and oversees commercially-sponsored football leagues for boys seven to fifteen years old, who compete in seven different divisions on the basis of age and weight. Founded as the Junior Football Conference in 1929 by Joseph J. Tomlin, it was renamed in 1934 after the legendary coach and innovator Glenn Scobey "Pop" Warner. Some of the Pop Warner alumni are quarterbacks John Elway, Joe Theismann, Randall Cunningham, and Rodney Peete. Others include Marcus Allen, Emmitt Smith, Drew Pearson, Lynn Swann, Dwight Clark, James Lofton, Dave Meggett, and Terry LeCount.

Six-Man Football

Six-man football is a variation of football with six players on a side, played (when possible) on a field eighty yards long and forty yards wide. The offense must advance fifteen yards, instead of ten, in four downs. Unless the ball is kicked or passed forward, it may not be advanced across the line of scrimmage until after a backward pass to a teammate is made by the receiver of the snap. All players except the passer are eligible to receive a pass. A field goal counts four points. A conversion try counts two points if place kicked or drop kicked and one point if made by a pass or run. The game is ended immediately when one team is forty-five or more points ahead at the end of the first half.

Touch Football

Touch football is played without protective pads, and the ball-carrier is downed not by tackling, but by a defensive player touching him with both hands below the waist (or sometimes anywhere between the shoulders and the knees).

Flag Football

Flag football is a sandlot game involving two teams of six to nine players. The ball-carrier can be "tackled" only by an opponent who removes a flag hung from the ball-carrier's waist or hip pocket. All players are eligible to catch a pass. The offensive team must score within four downs or they lose possession of the ball. The game is also called tail football.

Index